Spa

Veronica Heley

Sparrow

SCRIPTURE UNION
130 City Road, London EC1V 2NJ

First published 1984
Reprinted 1985

ISBN 0 86201 232 5

Printed and bound in Great Britain by
Cox & Wyman Ltd, Reading

1

Vivien was doing her homework when the doorbell rang. She glanced at the clock, thinking that her mother had forgotten her key that day, and went to open the door.

A policeman stood on the mat. He checked the number on the door and said, 'Is your name Forrester?'

'That's right,' said Vivien. Her long dark hair had slipped forward over her face, so she tossed it back. 'Do you want my mother? She'll be back in a minute, I expect.'

The policeman didn't answer directly. He said, 'Is your father home from work yet?'

Vivien gave him a pitying smile. 'I haven't got a father. Or rather, he doesn't live here. They got divorced when I was little, and he lives down in London.'

'Have you his address and phone number?'

'It's in the phone book.' She reached for the phone book, and then paused, suddenly uneasy. Why all these question?

He said, 'Do you see him often?'

She frowned. She didn't understand why he needed to ask these questions. She said, 'No, I don't see him often. Sometimes in the holidays, that's all. Is there something wrong?'

'How old are you, miss?'

'Fourteen and a half.'

The policeman was looking at her in an anxious way. She began to feel anxious, too. Her mother ought to have been home long before this.

She said, 'Has something happened to my mother?'

The policeman asked if there were anyone in the block of flats whom she knew well. . . .

And then Vivien knew that something terrible had happened to her mother, and that nothing was ever going to be the same again.

Ten days later Vivien stood in the middle of the living-room of the flat, and wondered if she were going to be sick. She had often felt sick during the last ten days, and now she was going to have to take a long car journey, and she wasn't a good traveller.

Her father came out of the bedroom with a cardboard box full of Vivien's records and cassettes.

'That's the last,' he said. 'Come along, Chicken. We'd best get cracking, or we won't be home in time for supper.'

Vivien wanted to protest about being called Chicken, but her voice wasn't behaving very well, so she didn't say anything. She went over to the piano – her own, much-loved piano – and stroked the sheeny, shiny surface. That piano and her oboe were the most precious things in the world to her, now that her mother was gone.

Her father said in a cheerful voice, 'Now don't you fret about the piano. They're collecting it in the morning, and it will be with you again by the weekend . . . though I don't know where we're going to put it. . . .'

Vivien turned to take one last look at the flat. The sun was brilliant across the carpet which she had chosen with her mother last year. The walls showed brighter patches where the bookshelves and pictures had been, for as long as Vivien could remember. Most of the furniture was to be sold, for her father had a house full of his own furniture down in London, and there wouldn't be any room there for these old bits and pieces.

Vivien picked up her oboe case and walked to the door. There she hesitated, despite her father's impatience to be off.

She said, 'I ought to have been having my oboe lesson this afternoon after school.'

'Yes, yes,' said her father. 'That's all been dealt with, and they'll fix you up with some lessons at your new school. Don't worry.'

She wasn't worrying, exactly.

She was in a state of feeling nothing. She hadn't cried since the policeman told her that her mother had been killed. A lorry had gone out of control coming down a hill and crashed across a pavement into a shop, killing her mother and injuring five other people.

One day Vivien had been going to school in her neat blue uniform as she had done every day since she was five, and the next she was cut off from everything she had ever known.

She had been going to a small private girls' school. Her mother was secretary to the managing director of a manufacturing firm in the Midlands, earning a good salary. Outside office hours, Mrs.

Forrester had devoted all her time and money to her musical daughter, giving her the best music teachers, and choosing to send her to a private school so that she need not mix with the rougher types of children.

Vivien had made many good friends at school. Two of them had come round after the accident and said how sorry they were. Vivien couldn't believe that she would never see any of them again . . . the other members of the school orchestra . . . the choir . . . the netball team . . . her own special friends in class.

Perhaps, she thought, it had all been a bad dream, and she would wake up in a moment, when the alarm went off as usual, at half-past seven.

She got into her father's estate car, and did up the seat-belt. She hoped, fervently, that she was not going to disgrace herself and be sick on the journey.

Her father was salesman for a big furniture company, and he had a company car. The back of the car was filled with Vivien's belongings.

Mr. Forrester drove fast and well. He turned on the radio, and found a light music programme which he thought Vivien would like. He also said Vivien would be sure to feel at home in London, because his twin boys were having piano lessons, too.

They were leaving the town . . . her home town . . . the town in which she had been born, and in which she had lived all her life. There was no one about to wave goodbye to Vivien. All her friends would be at school at that time of day.

Vivien turned her face to the window, and wondered what mark she had got for her last music essay. She had read it out to her mother, who had said she thought it ought to get an A. But Vivien would never know, now.

They stopped at a motorway service station for a cup of tea. Mr. Forrester asked if Vivien would like anything to eat, but she shook her head.

He said, in his comfortable way, 'You're too thin. Your new mother will have to fatten you up. It's a pity you never met Penny before. It would have made things easier. But there; I'm sure you'll get along just fine.'

Vivien had never met Penny because Vivien's mother had not wanted her to do so. Twice a year Penny took the children by the second marriage to stay with grandparents, and then Vivien would go away for a few days alone with her father, to the seaside.

Vivien had never seen her father's house in London, or heard much about the brothers and sisters of the second marriage. Now she was going to live with them.

Mr. Forrester was a big, sandy man, who nearly always looked good-tempered. He wore light brown suits and cream shirts, and there was a gold signet ring on the little finger of his left hand.

He said, 'Now look here, Chicken, I know it's going to be rough on you for a while. You'll be missing your mother, and you'll have to make a fresh start at a new school. It's bound to be difficult.'

'Yes,' said Vivien. She had asked what the alternative would be, and knew it would mean living in a children's home. She supposed that anything was better than that.

'Of course,' said Mr. Forrester, 'you'll have to

share a room with Sausage, that's your little sister. She's seven, and a right little tearaway!' His voice grew warm, when he spoke of his small daughter.

'Oh, Daddy, do I have to share a room?' She had not foreseen this.

'I'm afraid you'll have to, Chicken. At any rate for the time being. Maybe we'll be able to build another room on, later. The house is bursting at the seams already, with so many kids running loose! Baby is moving in with us, and you'll take Baby's place in Sausage's room. The Toads have their own room, of course, and woe betide anyone who goes in there uninvited!"

He chuckled.

Vivien hunched her shoulders. How could he laugh, when she was so miserable? And how much she disliked his habit of giving everyone a nick-name! Vivien hadn't been brought up to nicknames, and she didn't understand how anyone could like them.

She asked, 'Why do you call them the Toads? I know they're twin boys.'

'What? Eh? Oh, you'll see.' He looked at his watch, and said they'd best be getting along.

It was just like him to be in a hurry. Her mother had said he'd been in a hurry since the day he was born. Her mother had also said that one day he'd been in such a hurry to get promotion he'd moved away to a new territory and forgotten he'd left his wife behind. Vivien sighed. She could well believe it of him. He'd probably given his children nicknames because he'd forgotten what they were really called.

She got back into the car, and closed her eyes. She wished she were dead. She'd never shared a room with anyone, in all her life. She was sure she wouldn't be able to sleep, if she had to share a room.

Life was just too awful for words!

They came off the motorway, whizzed through suburban streets, and turned into a tree-lined road. It was a busy road, with a lot of traffic on it. The houses seemed very close together, to someone who had been brought up in a spacious country town.

Mr. Forrester turned the car into a cul-de-sac and drew up outside a large, semi-detached house. The house was neat with new paint, but the garden looked as if a horde of elephants had recently passed that way.

Vivien got out, stiffly. She felt shaky from the car journey, and still rather sick. She held on to her oboe case as if it were the only solid thing in a world that was melting around her.

The front door of the house opened and twin boys of about eleven shot down the steps to greet their father. One jumped on to his back, and hung there. The other pretended to be an aeroplane, and made zooming noises as he circled round them.

'Down, Toad!' said Mr. Forrester. He swung the boy round, threw him into the air, and caught him again before setting him down on his feet.

'Quiet, Toad!' he said to the other boy, who took not the slightest notice, but started to home in on Vivien without actually looking directly at her.

Vivien felt a lump in her throat, and stood up very straight, her knees pressed close together. She looked a forlorn figure in her navy blue raincoat, tightly belted around her thin figure.

A stout little girl in a stained T-shirt and grubby shorts wandered out of the front door, put two fingers into her mouth, and produced an ear-piercing whistle.

Vivien felt the noise go right through her head, and shivered.

'Zoo-om!' The Toad who was pretending to be an aeroplane flicked the end of Vivien's nose in passing. Vivien recoiled.

Mr. Forrester yelled into the house. 'Penny, we're here!'

'Just a minute!' A harassed voice floated out from the house, to the accompaniment of a baby yelling its head off. An untidy brown-haired woman appeared, jogging a baby in her arms.

Mr. Forrester kissed his wife, and the little girl – Sausage – gave another of her whistles.

Then he turned to Vivien. 'Come along, Chicken! Don't be shy! Come and meet your new family!'

2

Vivien felt as if she were going mad. Or deaf. The flat had been a quiet place, and it hadn't prepared her for this.

In the flat Vivien had had to be careful how loudly she played when she practised the oboe or piano. Down here no one seemed to care that the radio was blasting away in competition with the television set.

Everyone talked through, or yelled at each other, over the noise. Vivien noticed they didn't even bother to turn the sound down when the phone rang.

She blinked, trying to adjust to the noise. There seemed to be just one big living-room downstairs, with a door leading off it to a large square kitchen. Apparently the family ate at a table in the kitchen, and did everything else in the living-room. There was a wigwam in the middle of the floor, and you had to tread carefully or you'd foul the rails of the train set. Comics, books and newspapers littered the chairs. The cushions which ought to have been on the chairs were on the floor, and the children seemed to sit on them for choice.

'You must be tired and hungry,' said Penny, smiling down at Vivien. She dumped the baby in a corner of the settee, and held out her hand to Vivien. 'Come up and see your new bedroom, and then we'll all have something to eat.'

The plump little girl called Sausage tugged at Penny's skirt. She was looking at Vivien without friendliness.

Sausage said, 'Does she have to come in with me?'

'Now we've been into all that before,' said Penny, giving Sausage a push. 'Go and help the Toads bring Vivien's things in from the car.'

Sausage stood her ground. 'There's no room for her things in my room!'

'Yes, there is!' snapped Penny.

The baby began to howl again. Penny picked her up, and led the way up the stairs. 'Come along, Vivien. I'll show you your room, and then send the Toads out for some fish and chips for supper. You like fish and chips, don't you?'

'Yes, thank you,' said Vivien, but felt alarmed. She did like fish and chips, of course. Everyone liked fish and chips. It had been a treat for Vivien and her mother to have fish and chips on special occasions.

But Vivien had just had a long car journey, she had been feeling off colour for days, and she wasn't sure whether she could face fish and chips at the moment or not.

However, she followed Penny up the stairs, across a landing, and into a square bedroom. One large window overlooked an untidy garden at the back of the house. There was only one proper bed in the room and that was placed in the best light near the window. Above and around it on the wall there was some complicated shelving, crammed with books, records and toys.

On the inner wall there was a small wardrobe and a camp bed. By the camp bed there was a chest of drawers with one empty drawer half way out. On the side wall there was a folding table and a chair. Both overflowed with Sausage's clothing.

The walls were hung with a Snoopy wallpaper, and the curtains matched, as did Sausage's duvet and pillowcase.

It was a child's room, and Vivien felt far too old for it.

'There's your drawer and there's some space in the wardrobe for you,' said Penny. 'There's not much room here for your books and things, but we'll get Sausage to clear some of her toys out eventually. In the meantime we're putting up another bookcase on the landing for your things. Your father's ordered another bed for you, but it hasn't come yet. It'll be Monday before it will arrive now. You can manage till then, can't you?'

'Yes, thank you,' said Vivien, and sat down on the camp bed. She was still clutching her oboe case. She was filled with horror. There was no place for her to put any of her things out, and what was going to happen about her music centre, which took up a lot of space . . . and where could she set up her music stand in order to practise the oboe?

She felt tears well up inside her, and blinked. She must not cry yet. Not with Penny looking on. The baby started to yell again.

Penny said, 'Dumpling's hungry. I'll have to see to her, or she'll give me no peace. You'll be all right now, won't you?'

Penny vanished. Vivien made no attempt to get off the bed, or to take off her coat. She wondered where the bathroom was, and if she really was going to be sick, but was too tired to explore.

Sausage sidled into the room. She looked cross.

She said, 'This is my room.'

'Yes,' said Vivien. 'I know.'

'So long as you realise you mustn't touch any of my things, that's all right.'

Vivien wanted to say that it would be difficult to move without disturbing something of Sausage's, but she kept her mouth shut. She was too tired to argue.

Sausage plumped herself on the bed, and turned on a small portable radio. She fiddled with the knobs till she got Capital Radio, full blast.

Vivien closed her eyes, and wished she could die.

She slept badly, uneasy on the frail camp bed. When everyone got up in the morning, Vivien put on her old school uniform, brushed out her long hair till it hung smooth about her shoulders, and went down to breakfast.

Her face in the mirror looked peaky. She had always been thin, and since her mother died had hardly been able to eat anything. She hadn't been able to face fish and chips last night, and she couldn't eat much of the fried eggs and bacon Penny put in front of her at breakfast time.

Her father kissed them all goodbye and dashed off. He would be away for the rest of the week so it was no good thinking he might be of help in settling into this strange new world.

Then Penny put the baby into its pram, and they all set off to walk to school. Half way there the twins and Sausage waved goodbye and turned down the avenue which led to their school.

'There we are!' said Penny, gesturing across a wide, busy road. 'That's your new school.'

'It's very big,' said Vivien, thinking of her own private school, in its tree-shaded grounds.

'It's the biggest school for miles,' said Penny. 'We're to go straight to the office and you'll do some tests to see which sets are best for you.'

'What are sets?'

'I don't know much about it, dear. I think it means that you take O levels if you're in the top sets, and CSEs if you're in the lower sets. Your father told them you're pretty bright, so I don't suppose you'll have any difficulty finding your level.'

'I don't feel very well,' said Vivien. 'Do I have to start school today?'

She hadn't liked making excuses, because she knew how bad they would sound. She was pretty sure Penny wouldn't listen, and she didn't.

'Nonsense, dear,' said Penny, and wheeled the pram across the road, with Vivien hanging to it. The baby was asleep, for once. Vivien felt weird; sort of floaty and at the same time rather sick.

'It's awfully big,' said Vivien, as they went through iron gates into the complex of buildings which made up Fairfield Comprehensive School.

The school buildings sprawled over a large area, with passages connecting different blocks of classrooms. There were unexpected squares of garden here and there. At the back were playgrounds and playing fields and an enormous Sports Hall.

In Vivien's old school the children stayed put in their classrooms nearly all the time, with the teachers visiting them in turn. The children left their classrooms only to go to the science block, or for P.E.

In a comprehensive school, the system was different. Each child was allocated to a form room, where he or she went to register first thing in the morning.

After that they moved from one classroom to another. They went into the English section for English, and then came out at the end of the lesson. They went into the languages section for French or German, and out. They went into the science laboratories for science, and the history rooms for history. They were always on the move between classes, and because the school sprawled over such a large site, they sometimes had to travel considerable distances between classes.

Penny took Vivien to the office at the entrance to the school, and handed her over to one of the secretaries. Penny was in a hurry to get to the shops and couldn't stay.

The secretary looked at Vivien, and said, 'Oh, dear. Mr. Bird's been called away to deputise for the Head, and I know he wanted to see you, himself. We're all at sixes and sevens today, because of the exams, but I'll see if I can find out who's supposed to be dealing with you.'

She spent some time on the phone, apparently having little success, while Vivien sat on the edge of a chair and felt like a parcel in a Left Luggage Office.

Finally the door burst open and a woman with flashing glasses came in. She seemed to be in a hurry, and looked cross.

She said to Vivien, 'Wait a minute. I'll have to get hold of your papers.'

As Vivien hadn't moved, she thought that was a bit off. The newcomer argued with the secretary about taking charge of Vivien. The secretary seemed dubious about it, and Vivien felt she agreed with the secretary. The woman with glasses was a type of teacher easy to recognise; bossy, and quick-tempered. Vivien had had a Maths teacher once just like that.

'There's no one else free,' said the woman in glasses, with the air of one delivering a knockout. 'You know we're all up to our eyes at the moment, what with the exams and three of us off sick. I'm the only one who can fit the new girl in, so if you'll kindly hand over her papers. . . .'

'I think Mr. Bird must have them with him,' said the secretary. 'I know he wanted to see the new girl himself. He told me he'd spoken to the Head of Lower School about her, and they'd worked out a tentative time-table, but. . . .'

'Well, he's invigilating at an exam this morning, and can't leave. I'll give Vivien her test, and get the timetable from him later. Come along, Vivien.'

Vivien followed. She was put in a small room, given various sheets of papers with questions on them, and left to herself.

The room was quiet at first, and Vivien settled down to the questions, which looked easy enough. Then a bell rang and hordes of children stampeded along the corridor outside. There was a lot of shouting, and what sounded like a fight. Then everything became quiet again.

But Vivien's nerve had gone. She started to shake. She didn't know why she felt so bad, but she couldn't stop shaking. Then she realised she'd done a really stupid thing. At the top of the first sheet of questions, where she'd been asked to fill in her name and address, she'd put her old address, where she'd lived with her mother, and not her new address in London.

She crossed through the old address quickly, and her pen went slashing across the top sheet of paper, and on to the second, which was lying beside it. Vivien began to cry. She sniffed and felt for her handkerchief, but couldn't find one. Her mother had always seen to it that Vivien had a clean handkerchief when she left for school, but of course Penny had been too busy to think about such things.

The memory of her mother was so keen that Vivien felt she was hurting inside. She began to make slashing black lines and crosses all over the page of answered questions, and then she went on to do the same on the next sheet, and the next. She didn't know why she was doing it, but somehow it helped to ease the hurt inside her, to make big black marks on everything in sight.

When she'd filled the last sheet with black marks she put her head down on to her arms, and let the pen slip from her fingers. She was so tired. The clock ticked on above her head, and she slipped off into a doze.

She was awakened by the bell ringing again, and another stampede of children along the corridor.

The door opened and the woman came in. 'Well, have you finished?'

Vivien started awake, and looked with bleary eyes at her spoiled test papers. The woman picked them up, and looked through them. She drew in her breath with a hissing sound.

'I'm sorry,' said Vivien.

'Too hard for you, obviously,' said the teacher, jumping to conclusions. 'I thought you were supposed to be bright. Never mind. We'll pop you into one of the remedial classes. I think I know where we can find room for you.'

'Please,' said Vivien, beginning to understand that her future was to be decided on the basis of what she had failed to do in the last hour.

'Come along now,' said the teacher. 'You have just got time to settle in before lunch. Did you bring sandwiches?'

No, Vivien hadn't brought sandwiches. Penny had been far too busy to prepare sandwiches for them all.

'Can't I go home for lunch?' said Vivien, for the first time thinking with longing of her new home.

'No, of course not,' said the teacher, rapidly leading Vivien along corridors which all looked alike. 'You can get something in the canteen.'

The teacher opened a door and ushered Vivien into another classroom. Vivien took one look at the children, and moved her shoulders uneasily. These children weren't her type. The boys were well developed for their age, and so were the girls. That wasn't it. The point was that they all looked bored.

'This is Vivien Forrester,' said the teacher to a burly man at the blackboard. 'I think she'll be best off with you.'

Vivien heard the boy in the nearest desk snigger. The girl next to him muttered something about Vivien's 'posh' uniform, which was audible enough to make everyone around her laugh. Vivien's face grew hot.

The teacher in charge yelled 'Quiet!' There was

quiet for a moment, and then someone at the back whispered, 'Oh, don't we half fancy ourselves!' There was another outburst of sniggers, and Vivien wished the floor would open and swallow her up.

The school uniform at Fairfield consisted of grey sweaters and white shirts, over grey trousers or skirts. Vivien's blue uniform stood out in contrast, and it didn't help matters at all.

The teacher leafed through Vivien's spoiled exam papers and looked cross. He said, 'Hasn't the Dicky Bird seen her? She doesn't look remedial to me. She tackled these first questions all right.'

'Mr. Bird,' said the woman, laying emphasis on the Mister, 'is away today, and the office asked me to look after the new girl and put her in whatever class I thought fit. If she can't complete a simple test paper, she'd best come in with you. It won't do her any harm to go over basics again.'

'Oh, very well.' He turned up the volume on his voice, and yelled 'Quiet!' to the class.

They had been whispering together, but now they were quiet again. Vivien had never heard teachers shout at their class before. She jumped each time it happened. She felt that being in this class was like being put in with a cageful of lions, with the teacher as lion-tamer.

She was told to sit at an empty desk near the front, and share a reading book with the girl next to her. The lesson ground on its weary way. Hardly anyone in the class could read a sentence without stumbling. When it came to Vivien's turn, she read her sentence in a clear voice, making it obvious that she could do it, if no one else could. There were more nudgings about that, too.

When the bell rang at the end of the lesson, the teacher told Vivien to stay behind. He asked her a few questions about her previous schooling, and whistled between his teeth when she said she'd been hoping to take eight O levels in due course. He shook his head.

'What went wrong here?' he asked, pointing at the spoiled exam papers. 'You didn't try very hard, did you?'

She shrugged. She couldn't speak for tears in her throat.

He said, 'Well, speak up, girl!' And looked at the clock.

She couldn't. She tried to, but could only hang her head and hold on to the thought that the school day couldn't last for ever. Soon, surely, she would be allowed to escape and have her cry out in peace!

3

Vivien was met at the school gates at three o'clock by Penny, accompanied by a wailing baby in the pram. It was beginning to drizzle, and Penny was in a hurry to get home. The Toads and Sausage didn't come out till four o'clock, but they would need their tea as soon as they got back. Vivien got out at three because the school didn't give long break times during the day, but encouraged pupils to stay on after school for sport, drama, orchestra, and so on.

Penny did ask, in an absent-minded way, how Vivien's day had gone, but did not wait for an answer, which was just as well.

To Vivien, the day had been an unrelieved disaster, and she was not particularly anxious to talk about it. But after the first edge had been taken off their appetite, the Toads wanted to know which class she was in.

'It's not fixed yet,' said Vivien. 'They put me in one class. . . .' She didn't like to admit it was a remedial class, 'But two of the teachers said they didn't think I ought to be there, and they're going to do something about it.'

'Didn't you see Mr. Bird?' asked Penny, as she

spooned mush into the baby's mouth. 'Your father spoke to him about you, and told him how well you'd done at your old school. Of course, they'll have to give you a test, to make sure you're up to standard. I expect they'll do that tomorrow.'

'I did the tests today.' Here tears threatened again. 'But I didn't do them properly.'

'Why not?' said one of the Toads, reaching across her for the last biscuit.

'I bet she cried!' said the other Toad, looking disgusted. 'You can see she's been crying. I bet she messed it up.'

'Are you a cry baby?' enquired Sausage, with interest. 'I never cry. Not even when I fell down the stone stairs at school.'

Vivien's throat tried hard to let her speak, but nothing came out. To her horror, tears welled up in her eyes, and began to overflow. She pushed back her chair and ran from the room. As she banged the bedroom door behind her, she could hear the Toads roaring with laughter, and pounding on the table with their fists. 'Cry baby! She's a cry baby!'

Vivien heard Penny shout, 'Stop that!' Vivien buried her head under her pillow. She had thought she'd cried enough that morning to last a lifetime, but still the tears came, till she felt hot and soggy.

When she heard the door open, Vivien stiffened.

Sausage came in, and sat on her bed. Sausage was sucking her thumb, and looking at Vivien with round, shiny eyes. Everyone in the family had round blue eyes and light brown hair, except for Vivien. When they'd all looked at her at table, when they'd called her cry baby, she'd felt them all looking at her in exactly the same way – as if she were a freak.

Now Sausage leaned over to turn on her radio; she liked it loud.

Vivien screamed at Sausage. 'Turn that thing off!'

Sausage blinked, and turned the volume even higher. From below, Vivien could hear the television blasting away with the signature tune of Blue Peter, and from the kitchen at the back she could hear a pop song on the radio.

'I can't bear it!' Vivien sprang to her feet, and ran down the stairs. The Toads looked up from watching television, to stare at her with identical round blue eyes.

Vivien said, 'I hate you all!'

One of the Toads laughed, throwing his arms and legs about. The other mimicked Vivien, 'I hate you all!' in an affected voice.

'Vivien!' This was Penny, calling from the kitchen. Penny was elbow deep in washing-up water, and the baby was yelling in its high chair beside her.

'Vivien, come and help me, there's a dear! If you'll dry up these things, then I can get on with. . . .'

'Dry them up yourself!' flashed Vivien. She knew it was all wrong to lose your temper, but she simply couldn't help it. Everything was so horrible, and nothing was ever going to go right again, and she simply couldn't bear it.

She snatched up her raincoat and ran out into the roadway. It was raining hard by this time, but she didn't care. She ran and ran until she'd got a stitch in her side, and her shoes were like wet cardboard on her feet from splashing through puddles.

Finally she found a bus stop with a scrap of shelter from the rain, and huddled into it, shivering.

A bus came, looking large and friendly.

'Are you getting on this, dear?' said a stout woman behind Vivien.

Vivien shook her head, and let the woman pass her. The cold seeped up Vivien's legs, through her black tights. She hugged herself. Her long hair clung wetly to her shoulders and her cheeks. Two lads in the bus queue were carrying a transistor radio, playing pop music.

Vivien suddenly remembered her piano, which ought to be arriving in London soon. The thought of her piano made her feel better. Everything couldn't go on being as bad as it had been today. Soon she would have her piano again, and she would be able to resume her music lessons and everything would sort itself out. Why, perhaps tomorrow she'd have a music lesson at school!

She hadn't got a proper timetable yet. She'd gone from one classroom to the other with her remedial group that day, and in each case the teacher in charge had looked at Vivien, asked questions about her schooling, and looked baffled. Especially when it was obvious that she had mastered the three Rs some considerable time ago!

Two of the teachers had advised her to make an appointment to see Mr. Bird as soon as possible.

Tomorrow would be better, Vivien thought. It had better be!

She began to walk back home; luckily she had fled down a main road, so it was merely a case of following it back again till she got to the cul-de-sac. Penny was so preoccupied with the baby when Vivien returned, that nothing was said when she slipped back inside, and put her things on the radiator to dry. The twins were glued to the television, and Sausage was asleep in her bed, with the radio blasting away in her ear. Vivien turned the radio off, and fell into bed to sleep like the dead.

On her arrival at school next day, Vivien was given her own timetable.

Her form master, Mr. Carton, was a man with what seemed like permanent catarrh. His reddened eyes were never still, always roving around the classroom, ready to spot mischief and stamp on it before it developed into trouble. He would be taking Vivien for remedial maths.

Vivien studied her timetable with dismay. The worst thing about it was that there was no music, but a lot of the other lessons looked grim to her.

She looked round her class, and found a mixed bunch. Pupils were allocated to forms on the basis of first come, first served in the alphabet. Vivien Forrester came about half way along the eight form entry, and was therefore in 4L. Some of the pupils in her class were in the remedial set, and she recognised them from the day before. The others were strangers. She guessed that some would be in the top sets for everything, and the rest somewhere between O levels and CSEs.

The girl next to Vivien had permed hair and was painting her nails under cover of her desk. She took no notice of Vivien.

The boy on the other side was in Vivien's remedial class, and Vivien dropped her eyes when she saw he was leering at her. She wished herself back in her old school where she had known everybody, and everybody had known her.

At the end of form period, Vivien was due to move

out to the Art Building for Technical Drawing. Instead, she went up to the teacher's desk, and waited for permission to speak.

'Sir, my timetable,' she said. 'There's no music or French on it, and I'm supposed to be taking them for O level.'

He took the sheet from her with a sigh. 'There's no music or French because you're down for extra English or Maths. You need extra English and Maths lessons to pass your CSEs.'

'But I'm supposed to be doing O level Maths and English.'

'Look,' he said, glancing at the clock, 'I don't make out these timetables. The office does. You take it up with Mr. Bird, or with the Head of the Lower School, if you're not satisfied. Now off you go, or you'll be late for your next class.'

By this time all the rest of the class had disappeared. Vivien had no idea where to find the Art Department. She asked a girl who was running down the corridor, and she pointed vaguely in the opposite direction, so Vivien took that way.

Suddenly she stopped. The door beside her had a card on it, marked 'Music'.

Vivien looked up and down the corridor, but there was no one in sight, so she opened the door and went in.

Three girls and two boys looked round to see who had dared to disturb their lesson. They were all much older than Vivien. A middle-aged woman with a frown was taking the class.

'Yes?' she said, on seeing Vivien. 'What is it?'

Vivien lost her nerve. 'Sorry,' she said, and backed out of the room.

The corridor was still deserted. She looked this way and that. Tears threatened, but she refused to give way to them. Through the far door she could see a playground, capped with blue sky. That way lay freedom.

She pushed at the bar to open the door, and then hesitated. She had never played truant in her life before, and she felt bad about doing so now. She told herself that no one understood her, or cared about her. Mr. Carton had told her to take her problem to the office, but Vivien didn't know where the office was. He'd said she ought to talk to the Head of the Lower School; Vivien didn't even know his name.

She felt like an ant, in a strange ant-hill. She was only one small child in a school containing two thousand children. She felt it wouldn't matter to anyone if she walked out of school at that moment, so she did.

She looked about her. There was no one else in the playground. It had been raining again recently, and the ground was shiny black, and wet with puddles. She walked slowly round the nearest wing of the school buildings, and found herself in another playground. It was a bewildering place, this school. She hadn't realised how many playgrounds there were. This one was marked out for netball, and there were the posts, all ready for a game.

Vivien looked at the posts, and thought how happy she'd been in the netball team of her old school. Her mother had always come to watch Vivien play in matches.

Vivien hadn't known that they played netball here at Fairfield, and she didn't suppose they'd take any notice of her if she asked to join the team.

She felt in her pockets to see how much money she had. Penny had given her enough for a canteen meal, but Vivien wondered if it would stretch to a ticket for the cinema. If she was going to play truant, she might as well have something planned for the rest of the day.

Someone rapped on a window nearby. A woman's face appeared at the glass, and a hand beckoned to Vivien.

Vivien looked wildly about her. One of the teachers had spotted her, and was doubtless about to haul her over the coals for missing a lesson. She ran to the end of the playground, and found it a dead end. She was surrounded by walls with doors in them. One of the doors opened, and the woman came out.

4

The teacher looked at Vivien's blue uniform and said, in a not unkindly tone, 'I can see you're new. You shouldn't be in the playground now, you know. Did you get lost?'

'Yes, miss,' said Vivien, as the easiest way out of the situation.

'Show me your timetable. Where are you supposed to be?'

Vivien simply could not bear to be sent to do Technical Drawing.

'In the wrong place,' she said.

'What's that?' The teacher looked sharp. 'Are you being impertinent?'

Vivien sighed. 'I want to do music. I'm in the wrong classes.'

The teacher's eyebrows rose. 'It's nothing to do with me. You'd best see Mr. Bird, or . . . I forgot. He's away, isn't he?' She looked at her watch. 'Well, I'm in the middle of a class now, and I can't. . . .'

'Everyone's always too busy here,' said Vivien, stamping her foot. 'I wish I were dead!'

The teacher laughed, but she put her arm about Vivien's shoulders for a minute. 'My dear, it's not as bad as that, really it isn't. Now, come along with me, and I'll find someone to take you to the Art Department. If you really are in the wrong classes, you must take it up with the Head of Lower School, or with Mr. Bird when he gets back. Come along now. . . .'

'But I don't want to do Technical Drawing! I can't draw to save my life!'

The pressure about her shoulders increased. 'You don't know what you can do till you try. Come on, now. This is not the way to . . .'

Vivien burst into angry tears. She didn't really need to cry, but she guessed that if she did, she wouldn't be forced to go to Technical Drawing.

The teacher sighed. She didn't want to leave her class for too long, and it wasn't part of her job to deal with misfits. She led Vivien back into the school, detached a sensible girl from her own class to take the new girl to the medical room, and turned back to her teaching. But she made a mental note to talk to someone about Vivien at the next break period. She was not unfeeling; just busy.

In the medical room Vivien was given a cup of tea, some paper tissues, and told she might lie down and rest for a while. That suited her well enough. It was quiet in the medical room. She even dozed off for a while. When she woke up, she was shown the toilets, and then directed to the Office.

There was only one secretary in the Office, and she was up to her eyes in work. She listened to Vivien's story, and said it wasn't her place to interfere, and Vivien really ought to see the Head of Lower School about it, at the end of the afternoon.

'But what about music?' said Vivien. 'If I can't have music, I'm going home!'

'That bad, is it?' said the woman, but she laughed, and reached for her schedules. She found a music lesson set for that afternoon, and altered Vivien's timetable so that she could go to that instead of to Woodwork.

'But you must promise me,' said the secretary, 'that you won't try to play truant. Sometimes it's difficult to get the timetables exactly as we would like them straight away. This is a big school, and sometimes people have to do things they're not particularly fond of, but we do try to fit everybody in.'

'Oh, thank you!' said Vivien. She looked at the timetable. She was supposed to be in remedial Maths next. She tossed back her hair, and set off to find the Canteen. She was blowed if she was going to Maths, and she was hungry.

The canteen was a revelation to Vivien, who had been used to having no choice at all about what she ate at school. Here at Fairfield you could have a choice of salads and of hot things with chips. There was fresh fruit and cheese and puddings and biscuits and drinks of all kinds. Vivien had a good meal, despite an influx of younger kids, all pushing and shoving for places. Vivien wasn't used to children pushing and shoving like that, but she managed to get herself into a corner, and ate in peace.

Then she went off through the corridors searching for the Music room. There wasn't anyone in it at that time.

She looked at the piano. She sat down on the stool, and tried a scale, softly. The piano was in tune, and it was a good one. Vivien looked around her. There was nobody to stop her, so she began to play through some of her pieces.

She had been playing for some time when the door opened, and the next class came in. Vivien stopped playing, and looked around with a smile.

'Who are you, and what are you doing on the piano?' said the foremost girl. She was not smiling.

'I'm Vivien Forrester, and I'm to join the music class in period 7.'

'Nobody plays that piano unless Mrs. Wright gives permission,' said the girl, and slammed down the piano lid, narrowly missing Vivien's fingers.

'I'm sorry,' said Vivien. 'I didn't know.' She didn't wish to make trouble now that she was at last allowed into a music class.

'Well, now you do,' said the big girl. 'I'm the leader of the orchestra in this school, by the way. And of the choir. I'm doing music at O level.'

'So am I,' said Vivien eagerly. 'I play the oboe. I always played first oboe at my last school.'

There was a sudden frost in the air. 'I play first oboe here,' said the big girl. 'And my friend here plays second. We don't need any more oboes, thank you.'

While Vivien was digesting this news, the door opened and the teacher almost ran into the room, apologising for being late. Mrs. Wright had a lot to do. She was responsible for all the music in the school, with help from a music student now and then. She had an orchestra, a wind band and two choirs to look after, in addition to all her class work. She was also responsible for arranging music lessons with peripatetic teachers giving individual lessons, and for the musical evenings and plays performed for parents.

Most nights she stayed on at school after hours to take some kind of rehearsal, and she was always in a hurry.

When she heard that Vivien wanted oboe and piano lessons at school, and that she had expected to play oboe in the school orchestra, all Mrs. Wright could think of was that this was just another problem for her to solve.

'What a pity!' she said. 'We don't need any more oboes at the moment. You can't play another instrument, can you? What we really need is a bassoon player. Could you see what you can do with a bassoon? I'll get our bassoon out of the cupboard and you can take it home with you and practise.'

'But. . . .' said Vivien.

'As for lessons at school, well . . . I'll have to see what I can do about those, but at the moment we don't have anyone coming in who can teach oboe . . . or piano, either . . . however, if you can join the choir straight away . . . come to the rehearsal straight after school today . . . and if you could help out with the percussion sometimes. . . .'

'No, thank you,' said Vivien, feeling stiff and awkward. If she couldn't play her beloved oboe, she was certainly not going to be fobbed off with anything else! The percussion group, indeed! Everyone knew it was the lowest form of life in the orchestra!

The big girl broke in, with a malicious smile, to say that Vivien had been playing on the piano when they arrived.

'You mustn't do that, dear,' said Mrs. Wright. 'That's a good piano, and I don't allow beginners anywhere near it. When you've got through one or two exams, and I can see you're serious. . . .'

'I've got my grade V piano,' said Vivien, 'and I'm working on my Grade VI. I was supposed to have taken the exam last week, but we moved so I couldn't. And I've got my Grade VI in oboe, and I'm working for Grade VII.'

'Oh, really?' Mrs. Wright focused properly on Vivien for the first time. 'Well, now. That's different. Come and see me after school, my dear, and we'll talk about it. Now, let's get started on some work, shall we?'

'Show off!' hissed the big girl, as they went to their seats.

Vivien went red. She hadn't meant to show off. It had just slipped out. And now it looked as if she'd made an enemy of the girl who mattered most in the music world of the school.

Vivien bit her lip. The lesson was tough enough for Vivien to have to concentrate on what was happening but at the end of it, she felt she simply could not face going on to remedial English as she ought to have done. What good was remedial English to someone who was supposed to be studying Shakespeare's plays?

So when everyone tumbled out into the corridor and shot off in different directions, Vivien lingered in a corner and then slipped into the library. The library was a quiet place with carpets on the floor, and lots of bays where older pupils were studying in silence.

Vivien found herself an Agatha Christie, and settled down to read it. No one seemed to be curious about her, and for the first time since she'd entered the school gates she felt reasonably happy.

When the bell went for the end of the school day, she got up with reluctance. She wasn't looking forward to returning home to all that noise. The baby was teething, and Penny was always asking Vivien to help with the housework. Vivien had been rather spoilt up till now, for her mother had not expected her to help about the flat. Vivien felt a pang of loneliness.

Then she brightened. She was hungry, and at least Penny prepared big meals for them to eat. In fifteen minutes she could be tucking into cake and crisps and biscuits. . . .

'Hold hard!' A large hand grabbed her shoulder, and brought her up short. 'And where do you think you're going, may I ask?'

5

It was her form master, Mr. Carton, and he was looking grim.

He sneezed, blew his nose, and said thickly, 'You've been playing truant, haven't you?'

Vivien swallowed. 'Not really, sir.'

He pushed her along the corridor before him. 'Not really!' he echoed, in a sarcastic voice. 'You didn't turn up for Technical Drawing, nor for my Maths class. Someone saw you wandering around in the playground at one point. You may have been able to walk in and out of lessons as you chose at your private school, but you can't do that here.'

She bit her lip. 'I had permission from the Office to go to Music . . .'

'Did you explain that to anyone else? Young lady, you are here to learn, and like it or not, we are here to make sure that you do.'

'Remedial English and Maths won't teach me anything!' Vivien's temper was aroused, and she was prepared to argue.

'So-o! We think we're above doing a spot of hard work, do we?'

'My father explained to the Deputy Head that I was to go on with my O level studies.'

'Let me tell you something. Lots of parents think their children are budding geniuses, when they're hardly capable of adding two and two. If you've been put in the wrong classes, we'll soon find it out. But one thing I want to get straight, and that is that I'll stand no nonsense from anyone.'

'No, sir,' said Vivien. Inwardly she was seething, but she tried not to show it.

'Right. Then you'll do detention today, to ram the point home.'

'But . . .' said Vivien, alarmed.

Mr. Carton threw open the door of the Lower School Hall, and pushed Vivien inside, saying 'Here's another for the slave ship!'

About a dozen children were tangled in a mock fight in the centre of the hall. Vivien wanted to run away, but didn't dare open the door behind her, in case Mr. Carton was waiting to catch her.

Detention! She'd never had detention in her life before! At the old school it was considered a terrible disgrace to get detention. It was mentioned on your reports, and your parents were spoken to about it. What would happen if Penny were to be called to the school about Vivien's naughtiness, after only two days at school?

Vivien felt she would die of shame.

The door was flung open, and a hairy man bounced in, jacket flapping. As if pulled apart by strings, the fighting tangle of children separated and shot to seats at the side of the hall.

'That's it!' said the newcomer, rolling his eyes at them. 'No more nonsense from you lot, or you'll get what for! I've beaten up more bad children than you've had hot dinners!'

These ferocious words were delivered in not unfriendly fashion, and most of the children smiled. But Vivien, sunk in misery, shivered. What kind of teacher threatened his pupils with beatings?

'Hello!' said the teacher, stopping in front of her. 'You're new, aren't you?'

'Yes, sir,' whispered Vivien, wondering if he were going to hit her straight away.

The newcomer tapped his forehead, under the shock of greying hair. 'Wait a minute,' he said. 'Are you the one who's been upsetting everyone by walking in and out of classes as you think fit?'

'Yes, sir,' admitted Vivien, feeling herself damned beyond redemption.

'Come and see me at the end of detention. I've got to keep my eye on this lot all the time, you know.'

He went to a table, slammed down some exercise books, and began to correct them. There was silence in the hall, except for the whisper of pages of books and comics being turned now and then.

Vivien took a chair, but didn't get out her book. She wished she could have a heart attack and die, there and then. She was in trouble at school, she hated her new home, and nobody cared whether she lived or died!

She would run away. Only there was nowhere to run to.

Her father didn't really care about her, or he wouldn't have put her in this dreadful school, or made her share a room with Sausage.

If only her mother. . . . No, she would not cry. She would not!

If only there was someone to turn to, for help!

'Stuffy in here,' remarked the teacher. He opened a window above him, and returned to his marking.

Something crawled up Vivien's spine, and tingled at the base of her neck. Through the newly-opened window came the sound of fresh young voices singing. The voices were singing in harmony. They soared up to the sky and hung there, delicately changing chords. The choir was practising nearby.

Vivien knew the music, for she had it on one of her mother's records. What was more, she had sung it at her old school. She knew the words, too.

'Lift thine eyes, O lift thine eyes to the mountains, whence cometh help. . . . Thy help cometh from the Lord, the maker of heaven and earth. . . .'

It was one of the choruses from Mendelssohn's Elijah.

Unbidden, other words came into Vivien's mind. . . . 'Be not afraid, Thy help is near. . . .'

Those words came from the Elijah, too. How often her mother had played that record, and they had gone to hear a performance at the Town Hall only the month before the accident.

The voices outside died away in confusion, and some laughter. Vivien remembered that there was a nasty couple of bars there. She felt a leaping in her body. If only she could have been with the choir, she could have helped to put that bit right, because she knew just how it went.

She remembered that Mrs. Wright, the music teacher, had asked Vivien to join the choir, and to go to see her after school. Vivien had sulked in the library instead of going to her lessons, and thus destroyed her chance of joining the choir.

'Lift thine eyes. . . .'

The words hung in her mind.

She supposed that some people might take the words literally, and begin to pray. Vivien thought that it wasn't going to help her, to pray. After all, she hadn't been to church for ages. She'd gone to Sunday School when she was little, but the old vicar had retired and the new man had changed everything, so she'd stopped going. Her mother went sometimes, but Vivien had excused herself because she said she had so much practising to do.

Vivien told herself that God wouldn't be interested in her, anyway. Suddenly she remembered the old vicar, in one of his talks to the children, saying something about not even a sparrow falling to earth, without God knowing about it. 'And that,' the vicar had said, 'means you . . . and you . . . and you.'

Could it really be possible that someone . . . even someone as distant and remote as God . . . might really still care about her?

One part of her said that there probably wasn't a God, and that if there was, he wouldn't be interested in a little girl who had stupidly got herself into trouble.

The other part of her said, 'Well, why not try praying, and see what happens?'

She tossed back her hair, and thought about it. She decided she would try it sometime, but not now because she wasn't in church, or kneeling down.

'Lift thine eyes . . .' The choir were taking it from the beginning again.

Vivien lifted her eyes, and blinked. The hall was two storeys high, and because it was so high, there were beams crossing from one wall to the other high up, and other beams coming down from the roof. One of them made a perfect cross.

Vivien felt another tingle at the base of her neck. She had lifted her eyes, just as the music had told her to do, and she'd seen a cross. So she could pray if she felt like it.

'Well, I think that's enough of that!' said the master, gathering his books together. 'Off with you, all of you – and don't let me see you in here again!'

Everyone was going. Vivien panicked. 'Please, God, if there is a God. Please, help me!'

She got off her chair. Her leg had gone to sleep, and she stumbled.

'Hey up!' said the master, looking down at her from his great height. He dug into a pocket and brought out a bag of peppermints. He offered one to Vivien, and took one himself.

He said, 'I remember the time I first had to walk into a comprehensive school. I'd been at a small village school before. I thought I'd been dropped into the anteroom of hell.'

Vivien smiled, politely.

He said, 'You mustn't let it get you down, you know. Everyone feels bewildered at first. You'll soon find your feet. I hear you think you've been put in the wrong class. Someone said you were doing O level work before. What English books were you doing?'

She told him, and he nodded.

He said, 'We're doing the same syllabus here. Did you understand the books? Which one did you like best?'

'The George Orwell. But I liked all of them, in different ways.'

'Someone said you hardly touched your test paper. Why was that?'

He really seemed to want to know. Suddenly her eyes flooded with tears again. She couldn't talk, or do anything but fumble for a non-existent handkerchief.

'Whoops!' said the teacher. 'Did I press the wrong button?'

She shook her head. He was being so unexpectedly nice, and she must try to explain. 'I was silly. I cried, and then I went to sleep, instead of doing the papers. It wasn't that they were too difficult, or anything.'

'Why did you cry? Because you found the school bewildering?'

She shrugged. 'Everything's just awful. At home, and here.'

Someone opened the door of the hall and yelled to them to hurry up.

'Help!' said the teacher, glancing at the clock. 'Look, I'm due to take a group of children up to the West End in the minibus, to see a play . . . I've got to dash . . . but I don't like to leave you . . .'

'I'll be all right,' said Vivien, sniffing.

'Sure?'

'There's just one thing. Will this detention go on my report? Will my father have to hear about it?'

He burst out laughing, and he had a big laugh.

'No, of course not! Come on, child; smile! It's not the end of the world, you know!'

He put his arm about her shoulders, and shepherded her to the door. She ran out into the corridor, collected her coat from the empty cloakroom, and then went home.

6

Her father had come home, and everyone was talking at once – except for Vivien. She sat silent in a corner and wished herself elsewhere.

The Toads were telling their father about some piece of mischief that they'd done at school. At the same time Sausage was telling him everything she'd had to eat since he'd left. The baby was wailing, of course, and Penny was despairingly trying to tidy the room.

Penny had asked Vivien to help a couple of times, but Vivien didn't feel like it. She didn't see why she should help to clear up a mess which she'd not made. Why shouldn't the Toads and Sausage clear up their own mess?

Finally Mr. Forrester said 'Enough!' in a voice like the teachers, and everyone laughed and turned down the volume. Only then could you hear that the telly and the radio were still blaring away in the background.

Mr. Forrester turned to Vivien and held out his hand to her.

'Well, Chicken?' he said. 'And how did you get on?'

Penny drew her hand across her forehead. 'That's

another thing. I'm going to have to take Vivien into town tomorrow morning, to get her new uniform. Could you look after Dumpling for me?'

One of the Toads picked his nose, and looked at Vivien with cold blue eyes. 'She's been put in with the dumbos.'

'What?' said Mr. Forrester, bristling.

'Who told you that?' said Vivien, her colour rising.

'One of my mates has an elder brother at Fairfield, and he told me,' said the Toad. There was a nasty glint in his eyes. Vivien realised with a start of dismay that this Toad disliked her as much as Sausage did. It made her feel weak and stupid, when people disliked her.

'Is this true?' said Mr. Forrester, looking at Vivien.

Everyone was looking at Vivien. She considered lying down on the floor, and having hysterics. That way everyone might get to be sorry for her, instead of being cross with her all the time.

She thought, Please God . . .

Somewhere deep inside her, a small voice said, 'Be not afraid, thy help is near. . . .'

She stood up, and took a deep breath. She said, 'I messed up the entry papers, and they put me in the remedial class for the time being. But I'm supposed to be seeing someone about it on Monday.'

'That's ridiculous!' Mr. Forrester exploded. 'I told that fool of a Head quite clearly. . . .'

'It was my own fault,' said Vivien, trying to keep calm. 'I was tired and upset and felt sick, and I just messed it up.'

'Why were you tired and upset?' demanded Mr. Forrester. Then he realised what he'd said, and bit off his anger. He turned to look at Penny.

'Don't look at me,' said Penny, with a shrug. 'I've hardly seen the child. Every time I ask her to do anything for me, she disappears.'

Mr. Forrester rubbed his eyes with both hands, got up, took Vivien by the hand, and led her through into the small front room. This was his study. Vivien hadn't been in this room before. She'd been told that none of the children were allowed in, and she could see why, for there were papers and piles of catalogues and an electric typewriter in there. The Toads would have reduced the lot to a shambles in five seconds flat.

Mr. Forrester drew out chairs, and seated them both.

'Now then,' he said, 'let's have your side of it.'

Vivien burst into tears. She hadn't meant to. She'd have thought she simply couldn't cry any more, but she did. This time Mr. Forrester did the right thing. He pulled their chairs close together, and hugged his daughter. She was too big to sit on his knee, he said. At that Vivien began to giggle, because it was quite true and she really was too big to sit on anyone's knee.

'Well, now?' he said, when she had mopped herself up with his handkerchief.

'I hate it here,' said Vivien, in despair.

'Give it a chance. You've only been here a couple of days. Besides, what else can we do about it?'

She sighed. Nothing.

He said, 'What's the very worst thing?'

'The noise,' she said readily. 'And sharing a room with Sausage. How on earth can I do any music practice, or any homework, when she's got the radio on all the time? She hates me being in her room, anyway. I put my clothes on the chair last night, and she threw them off.'

'But Chicken . . .'

'And I really don't like being called Chicken.' She bit her lip. He was being so nice to her, and she had to spoil it by criticising him!

'Don't you, Chicken?' he said, absentmindedly.

Vivien had to laugh.

'What's up?'

'You still called me Chicken, even though I asked you not to.'

'Oh.' He thought about it. 'I like pet names. Don't you?'

'I'm not sure. We never had them, Mum and I.'

'No. Well, I'll try to remember, but it is difficult, you know. I mean, you couldn't call the Toads anything else but Toads, could you?'

Vivien shook her head. No, you really couldn't. As a matter of fact, she couldn't tell one from the other yet. She didn't even know what their real names were.

'Nor Sausage, either,' said her proud father. 'I mean, she just is a Sausage, isn't she?'

'I suppose so,' said Vivien with a sigh. 'But I'm not a Chicken, really I'm not.'

He surveyed her from head to foot, and said perhaps not. He bit his thumb, then said, 'How about our putting your piano in here and allowing you to do your music practice here, and your homework?'

Vivien gave a little jump in his arms, and looked about her. The room was not large, and it was crammed with office furniture.

He said, 'We could move some of my things upstairs into our bedroom, so that we could get the piano in. But you must promise me never to let the other kids in here. And of course when I need to work here of an evening, you'll have to work in the kitchen.'

'Oh!' Vivien flung her arms about him, and kissed his cheek.

He held her close for a moment and then he said, in a muffled voice, 'You are like your mother, you know. I ought to have remembered how she felt about noise and privacy. But you forget, you know. You forget.'

Vivien was silent. She wondered if her father really had gone off in a hurry one morning, and forgotten all about her mother. It didn't really seem possible to forget you had a wife and child. She wanted to ask him about it, but didn't quite dare to do so.

'All right now?' he asked. 'Do you think you can face life again now?'

She nodded.

'But promise me this,' he said, wagging his finger at her. 'You must help out in the house. I know you didn't do any housework when you lived with your mother, but this is different. Penny's got far too much on her plate, and you ought to help her whenever you can.'

'The others don't help,' said Vivien, turning sulky.

'They're young yet,' said her father.

'But. . . .!' said Vivien, prepared to argue about it.

'Now, then!' said her father, raising his finger at her. 'If you want special privileges in this house, you've got to pay for them. Right?'

'All right,' said Vivien. She wasn't going to throw away the chance of having a room to herself, by arguing with him.

'Now about your music lessons,' said her father. 'You're to have oboe lessons at school, but Penny's fixed up for you to go for piano lessons to a woman who teaches near here. She's been teaching the Toads for nearly a year now, and she's promised to fit you in as well. That'll be nice, won't it?'

'Oh yes. Thank you!' She stood up, feeling somewhat shy when she remembered how she'd thrown her arms about him, and kissed him. He seemed to feel shy now, too. He patted her shoulder, and asked if she'd help him get some of his books upstairs, so that she might have room to study that weekend.

One of the first things she came across in unpacking, was her mother's old Bible. Vivien sat down on the floor and leafed through it, trying to find that bit about the sparrows . . . and the bit from the Elijah. She seemed to remember there was also a nice verse saying that all the hairs of her head were numbered in God's sight, but she couldn't find that. She couldn't find the bit about the sparrows either, but she did come across a passage which her mother had underlined.

'Why do you look at the speck in your brother's eye, and pay no attention to the log in your own eye. . . .?'

She put the book down. Was there a log in her own eye?

Was that why she was so unhappy and hated everyone around her?

Perhaps she had been too critical of her new

family. Perhaps if she hadn't been prepared to hate them, they wouldn't have come to dislike her.

It was a hard thing to think about, but whatever else she was, Vivien was not a coward. She put the Bible on the top shelf of the bookcase which her father had cleared for her, and hastily stacked the other books beneath. She had promised her father that she would help Penny about the house that weekend, and she supposed she must do so.

She touched the Bible again before she left the room. She really must find that bit about the sparrows. . . .

Later that evening, when Sausage was asleep, Vivien slipped downstairs to rescue her Bible. She wanted to read it in bed, before Penny came up to see that all the lights were out upstairs.

* * *

In the morning they went to buy Vivien her new school uniform, and in the afternoon Penny handed the Toads their music, and sent them off with Vivien to their piano lesson.

The Toads seemed in no hurry to get there. Vivien was looking forward to the lesson so much that she would have gone ahead, if she had known the way.

'What's this piano teacher like?' she asked the Toads. 'I expect she'll notice that I haven't done any proper practice for a fortnight. I wish my piano had come! My scales are awful!'

One of the Toads shrugged, and kicked a stone clear across the road.

The other said, 'She's all right, I suppose. She gives us chocolate, and biscuits with cream in.'

'I think she's awful,' said his brother, kicking another stone.

'Why?' said Vivien. 'Is she so strict with you?'

Both Toads laughed.

Vivien said, anxiously, 'Does she rap your fingers with a ruler, if you keep on making mistakes? I know it's supposed to make you learn more quickly, but I hate it. My first piano teacher was like that, but the one I was with the longest . . . she was nice.'

'I'd give her a kick, if she rapped my fingers,' said one Toad.

'Well, what does she say when you don't practise?'

'Nothing. Well, she can't, can she? We haven't got a piano at home.'

'You mean,' said Vivien, 'that you go from week to week without practising, and she doesn't do anything about it?'

'What can she do, except complain to Mum, who can't do anything to us but yell that we ought to go next door to practise. That's what we're supposed to do. But we don't, usually. Unless she yells.'

'Well, my piano ought to be here any day now.'

'Don't tell her that!' said one of the Toads.

The other grinned. 'Silly! We're not allowed in the study, so we won't be able to practise on her piano, will we?'

'What's the point of your having lessons, if you don't get on?' said Vivien, in a bossy tone.

'Little swot!' said one Toad, quietly, to his brother.

Vivien's face burned, but she thought it best not to say anything.

Mrs. Kerno, the piano teacher, taught in her front room. The air was stale and smelt of cats. Vivien tried not to worry about sitting down in a chair which the cat had only just vacated. She liked cats, but she had her brand new skirt on, and was afraid it would collect ginger hairs.

Mrs. Kerno was a broad, bosomy lady with a comfortable face. She was drinking tea and eating biscuits when they arrived, and she put the plate between Vivien and one of the Toads while the other wriggled around on the piano stool and pretended he couldn't remember where to start his piece of music.

He played erratically, without enthusiasm, but Mrs. Kerno seemed pleased.

Vivien looked down at her shoes. The piano was flat, and out of tune. It wasn't just a little bit out of tune. It was horribly out of tune. Also, it had a jangly tone which grated on Vivien's ear.

She drew in her breath. Phew! Couldn't Mrs. Kerno hear that it was out of tune? But no, Mrs. Kerno was smiling and waving her hand, telling the Toad that he was a good little boy and could have two chocolates out of the box on top of the piano.

Vivien opened her eyes wide. She'd never heard of a piano teacher who bribed little boys with chocolate. She waited for Mrs. Kerno to put the Toad through some exercises, or some scales, but it didn't happen.

The first Toad got off the stool with the air of one released from the rack, and the second Toad took his place. The second Toad played fast and furiously, with his face all screwed up. He put the loud pedal down at the beginning, and didn't take it off till the end. He made a hideous noise.

Vivien waited for Mrs. Kerno to pull the boy up, but she didn't.

Instead, Mrs. Kerno smiled at Vivien over the boy's shoulder, and said it was nice to have three pupils from one family, wasn't it? 'Such musical boys!' she said.

'Yes,' said Vivien, faintly. She wondered who was fooling who. The second Toad was also given two chocolates, and made way for Vivien at the piano.

'I'm working for my Grade 6,' said Vivien. 'I keep going wrong on one of the scales, though.'

'I always think scales are so boring, dear,' said Mrs. Kerno, putting another chocolate into her mouth. 'Why don't you play me one of your pretty pieces?'

Vivien felt lost. She'd always been taught that unless you got your scales right, you'd get nowhere. She'd always had to start her lessons with her scales, to get her fingers going. Without scales, she'd been told, there was no hope of acquiring technique.

Vivien said, 'Could I just play you this one scale, where I go wrong all the time?'

She played the scale, her fingers flying up the keyboard, but hesitating half way down. She played it again, annoyed with herself. This time she got up and down, but ended on the wrong fingers. She tried it hands separate, and got it right. She tried it hands together again, and still the fingers came out wrong.

'You see!' she said. 'I make a mistake somewhere, but I can't see where.'

'Does it matter, dear?' said Mrs. Kerno, smiling and winking at the Toads. 'Why don't you play me a nice piece now?'

Vivien stiffened. Her pieces were not 'nice'. They

were difficult, they were crazy, they were wonderful. But they were not 'nice!' She began to wonder if Mrs. Kerno had any qualifications at all for teaching music.

'Beethoven, or Grieg?' asked Vivien, in a steely voice.

'Beethoven's so difficult, dear. Why not the Grieg?'

Now the Grieg piece was fiendishly difficult.

Vivien said, in a falsely sweet tone. 'Do you like Grieg's New World Symphony, or his Pastoral Symphony best, Mrs. Kerno?'

'Oh, the New World, dear.'

Vivien pushed back her stool and stood up. She stacked her music, and thrust it in her case. She was simmering with rage.

She said, 'You're an old fraud! I don't think you know anything at all about music! Dvorak wrote the New World Symphony, and Beethoven wrote the Pastoral. If you don't even know that. . . ! I'm certainly not going to have piano lessons from you! You've no more right to charge for piano lessons than . . . than a big, fat currant bun!'

7

'That's torn it!' said one of the Toads, as they walked home.

The other Toad was doubled up, laughing. He'd started laughing as soon as they left Mrs. Kerno's house, and he didn't seem able to stop.

'She is a fraud!' stormed Vivien. 'She can't teach the piano for toffee!'

'We know that,' said the Toad who was not laughing. 'But it makes Dad happy to think we're getting music lessons. He always wanted to play the trumpet when he was a boy, and kid brother here said he wanted to learn the piano . . . at first.'

'You mean,' said Vivien, 'that you knew she was no good, and you kept on going?'

'We didn't always go.'

Vivien gaped. 'But it must be costing your mother . . .'

'Old Kerno daren't charge much, or she wouldn't get any pupils at all. Besides, we reckon we get our money's worth in chocolates and biscuits from her.'

'Well, I can't learn from her,' said Vivien. 'What am I going to do?'

Two pairs of round blue eyes stared at her, and

this time they were almost sympathetic. Vivien noticed that one of the twins had pointed ears. Otherwise they still looked identical to her.

The one with the pointed ears said, 'You said you were good, and we didn't believe you. Sorry about that. The way you ran up and down those scales! It was ace!'

'High praise, brother!' said the other Toad, but he grinned at Vivien as he said it. 'Kid brother here wants to be a musician when he grows up.'

'Well, he won't if he stays with Mrs. Kerno,' said Vivien.

'Oh, I grew out of all that ages ago,' said the Toad, in an off-hand way. 'I expect I'll become a pop star, instead.'

'And I'll be your drummer,' said his brother, and began to turn himself into a one-man band, trumpeting and banging and blowing down the street.

Penny was very upset when she heard about the music lesson. She had been in a bad temper anyway, because Sausage had paid a visit to the fridge behind her mother's back, and eaten half the ice cream intended for supper. Now Vivien had been rude to Mrs. Kerno, who was a very nice woman, and had been so kind to the twins!

'How dare you say that Mrs. Kerno is no good as a teacher!' said Penny, near to tears. 'You come here and cause trouble wherever you go! You argue with the teachers, and get yourself a bad name at school! And now you've upset one of my dearest friends, and how I'm going to look her in the face again, I do not know!'

'I'm sorry,' said Vivien. 'But I know I'm right.'

'You always think you know best,' raged Penny, diving for the box of tissues. 'But you're only a child. . . .'

'Harrum!' One of the Toads cleared his throat. 'Sorry and all that, Mum, but she's right. Old Kerno's the pits. I've been meaning to mention it for some time now, but somehow it always slipped my mind.'

'Oh, get out of my sight, all of you!'

Penny threw the box of tissues on the floor, and sat down at the kitchen table to have a good cry. Vivien and the Toads looked at one another, and silently faded from the scene. It would be best to let their father deal with this one.

The battle about Mrs. Kerno raged backwards and forwards over the weekend. Vivien kept out of the way as much as possible, and when she had a minute she took out her Bible and went back to the Gospel of St. Luke, reading it from the beginning. When she got to the bit about not judging others, she stopped and had a good think.

Perhaps Penny was right, and Vivien was too critical of others. She'd certainly been rude. She ought not to have upset Mrs. Kerno like that. Perhaps Mrs. Kerno was good with little children, as Penny said. And then Vivien shuddered, remembering how badly the Toads had played, and thought that nothing could be worse.

But on the other hand, the Toads had learned something, even if they'd also picked up a lot of faults. Vivien sighed. Why was everything so difficult?

It was a relief to get back to school, even though there was a fresh set of problems to solve there. As

Vivien walked in through the school gates, she reminded herself yet again about not judging others. Penny was quite right in saying that Vivien had caused a lot of unnecessary trouble at school last week. She ought to have listened to what people were trying to tell her, and not jumped to conclusions.

She ought to have asked God to help her from the very beginning. She asked him to help as she walked through the playground. She asked him to help her not to be so hasty. She asked him to keep an eye on her that day, to keep her out of trouble.

Then she stopped short, struck by a sudden thought. She'd been almost, but not quite, saying the Lord's Prayer. She hadn't said that prayer for years. She'd almost forgotten how it went. There and then, standing in the playground, she said the age-old prayer in her mind.

The playground was a swirling mass of children who all seemed to know one another, but for the first time Vivien wasn't afraid or ill at ease.

She felt quite calm inside herself when the bell rang and they all went in to their form rooms. Vivien looked like the rest of the class now, in her neat grey skirt and white blouse.

Mr. Carton called Vivien out of class, and told her that Mr. Bird was still away, and so she must resign herself to going on with her existing timetable in the remedial classes. A little while ago Vivien would have burst out at that, and made a scene.

She wanted to argue, but a voice held her back, saying 'Who are you to judge?'

She looked up at Mr. Carton, and said, 'Do you think he'll be away long, sir?'

'No, no,' said Mr. Carton, wiping his nose. 'Now look,' he said, in a kindlier tone, 'we can't move you up into one of the top sets until we have some proof that you can deliver the goods. You did mess up your entrance papers, didn't you? Normally we'd have had some sort of report from your old school to go on, but I gather nothing's come through yet. Now I had a word with the Head of Lower School about you, and he says you're to go along to the office at break, and they'll let you have another go at the entrance papers. How does that grab you?'

Vivien gulped. 'Oh, thank you!'

'Don't thank me,' said Mr. Carton. 'Thank the Head of the English Department who was taking detention on Friday night. He seemed to think you were worth taking a bit of trouble over . . . the Lord alone knows why!'

Yes, thought Vivien, The Lord did know why. She went back to her desk feeling slightly stunned. Could everything come right, just because she'd sent up a prayer for help?

That night in bed Vivien did a lot of thinking about herself and the Bible, and the change it had made in her life. She'd been thinking in a woolly way about it for some days, but now she made a definite decision to follow Christ. She was beginning to realise that a lot of things in herself would have to change and she would need Christ's help to live up to what he wanted of her. She supposed it wasn't always going to be easy. Just look at St. Peter, she thought. But if he could fall down on the job and be forgiven, there's hope for me. Please God, help me to be a Christian here at home and at school, she prayed.

Then she turned over and went to sleep.

* * *

There was quite a bit of delay while Vivien was found places in the top classes. By the end of the week she was in the top set for English and French, and the second set for maths and German. The only major problem was music, because she couldn't fit in both history and music lessons, and the teachers didn't want her to give up history.

Because she'd made up her mind to do as the teachers asked, without arguing, Vivien got no music lessons at all that week. She'd gone to orchestra practice once, been handed the loathed bassoon, and thereafter ignored it. Mrs. Wright kept sending messages to Vivien, asking to see her after school, but Vivien felt she simply couldn't face another scolding, so she didn't go. She didn't go to choir practices, either, because that would have meant seeing Mrs. Wright again.

She didn't know what she was going to do about her music, which seemed to have come to a total standstill. Every night she read her Bible, and prayed for help. She even wrote a letter of apology to Mrs. Kerno. She felt a little better when she posted that off, but it didn't get her any nearer to having proper music lessons again.

The following Monday Mr. Bird returned to the school, and called Vivien into his office for their much delayed interview. He had an india rubber face which he often pushed around, and moulded with his fingers while he was talking. His eyes were kind and wise.

Vivien felt that he only had to take one look at her, to know all about her. She felt that if only he had been there when she arrived at the school, she wouldn't have had so many problems.

'Well,' he said, seating her in a comfortable chair, 'I hear you've had a chequered career since you arrived here.'

Vivien grinned, because he didn't seem to be blaming her for it.

He gestured to some papers on his desk. 'We've got the report from your old school through at last. They said some nice things about you.' He checked some schedules. 'I see you've ended up in the O level groups for everything, and that you've signed up for tennis practice, and want to go in for netball when they start up again next term. That's fine. There's nothing like keeping busy. Are you finding your way about the school all right now?'

'Yes, I only got lost twice this week. I got a map from Mr. Carton, and that helps.'

'So have you any other problem for me to solve?'

'It's music, sir. I want to be a musician when I grow up, but there's no place for me in the school orchestra, and they can't give me lessons here, either.'

He seemed to know something about it already. 'Ah, yes. Young Melanie plays first oboe, doesn't she? Well, Melanie has a lot of problems at home. . . .'

So have I, thought Vivien.

'. . . and she's worked very hard to get this far in the orchestra. She's earned her place there, so to speak.'

So have I, thought Vivien, thinking of her hours of

practice, and her pile of exam certificates. She opened her mouth to argue, but then she shut it again, thinking. . . . Help me, Lord.

'On the other hand,' said Mr. Bird, pushing his cheek up with his hand till he looked lop-sided, 'I hear they need a bassoon player in the orchestra.'

Vivien was silent. Vivien had taken the bassoon home, together with a book of simple exercises, given them both a thump, and shoved them under her father's desk in the study. She hadn't looked at them since, and had no intention of doing so, either. If she couldn't play her beloved oboe, then she wasn't going to play a silly old bassoon, instead!

'The bassoon is a very nice instrument,' suggested Mr. Bird.

Vivien thought of Mrs. Kerno, who looked rather like a bassoon herself. All round and plummy.

She began to giggle, and then stopped, because it wasn't funny at all, really.

'Yes?' said Mr. Bird. 'Tell me. . . .'

So she told him. She told him about her piano which was still on its way to her, and about her old music teachers and the orchestra in her old school; she told him about going for a music lesson with the Toads, hoping that Mrs. Kerno would be as good as her last teacher. She told him about the awful piano, and the way that Mrs. Kerno didn't bother with scales, or do anything but simple pieces, and how she'd got Dvorak mixed up with Grieg. . . .

'. . . and I thought she was simply awful, and I hated her, and I called her a fraud and a currant bun to her face. So now I'm in worse trouble than before, even though I've written a letter, apologising to her!'

Mr. Bird took out a handkerchief, and smothered his face in it. He made a sound something between a cough and a sneeze, wiped his nose with care, and returned his handkerchief to his pocket. His eyes looked runny, as if he were going down with a cold.

He said, 'I believe she's quite good with small children.'

'Hmph!' said Vivien. 'I'm sorry for anyone who goes to her!' She hadn't intended to argue, but she simply couldn't help it. 'She's only doing harm, you see. I mean, one of the Toads said he really wanted to learn at the beginning, but now he couldn't care less.'

'The Toads?'

'My twin brothers. Half brothers. They're awful, too.'

'What's the matter with them?'

'Well, they spend all their time getting into mischief, only nobody seems to mind, like they do with me. One of them gets these 'marvellous' ideas, and the other follows him.'

Mr. Bird pushed one side of his face up again, and his eyes went all chinky. He said, 'They're quite bright, I assume.'

'I should think so. I believe they're supposed to come to Fairfield in the autumn.'

Mr. Bird was a brave man, and he didn't blench. He did square his shoulders, however, and said he supposed the school could stand it.

'You may be able to,' said Vivien, 'but I'm not sure that I can.'

Instead of telling her off for impertinence, Mr. Bird said, 'That bad, is it?'

Vivien sighed. 'If it weren't for the sparrows, I'd give up.'

She expected him to look at his watch or the clock at that point, and tell her to go, but he didn't. He was the only teacher at Fairfield who didn't seem to be governed by the clock. He must have had a hundred important things to do, but he sat back in his chair and said, 'Tell me about the sparrows.'

'Well, you know. . . . "Not one sparrow is forgotten by God". I'm worth more than a sparrow, he said. I have to keep remembering it, though, especially in the playground.'

Mr. Bird swivelled round in his chair to look out on to the playground, which was teeming with children.

'Ah,' he said. 'I think I see what you mean. I should have said starlings, myself. Have you seen and heard the starlings flock in to roost in the City? They make a lot more noise than sparrows.'

'Yes, but Christ said sparrows.'

He pushed his face up and down again, and looked squinty. Then his face straightened out, and he said, 'So he did. I'd forgotten. Well, Little Sparrow, I want you to remember in future that we care just as much about the children here as he does. Maybe we can't sort out all your problems straight away, but we'll do our best. It's not easy. We've got children here of all shapes and sizes, and we've got to see what we can do to help all of them; not just the clever ones, but all of them. Do you understand?'

She sighed. She supposed she did. At her old school they were only interested in getting you through exams. Here it was more complicated, because a lot of the children were never going to pass even the simplest exam, but they could be helped to take their place in the world, by concentrating on other skills.

Mr. Bird pulled Vivien's timetable towards him, and made a couple of corrections on it.

He said, 'You'll have to cut out history, if you want to take music at O level. Is that all right with you?'

'Yes, sir.'

'And you must see Mrs. Wright about piano and oboe lessons. She ought to be able to fix you up with someone better than Mrs. Kerno.'

'I'm supposed to see her after school,' said Vivien. She sighed. She didn't really see what Mrs. Wright could do to help her, so what was the point of going to see her after school?

'Cheer up,' said Mr. Bird. 'And remember that someone's keeping an eye on you, always.'

'You?' said Vivien.

'Him,' said Mr. Bird, pointing upwards. 'And me as well, of course.'

8

The last lesson ground to a close, and Vivien had to decide whether to go straight home to help Penny with the supper, or go to see Mrs. Wright. Vivien had promised Penny that she would help that evening, but she didn't feel like it. Not one little bit.

She didn't feel much like going to see Mrs. Wright, either. There were bound to be questions about how Vivien was getting on with the bassoon, and Vivien didn't feel she could cope with another scolding. She felt she'd had enough scoldings to last her a lifetime.

As for piano and oboe lessons, there weren't any at school, and she might just as well resign herself to it.

Vivien was just about to pass the door of the music department when a voice inside her said, Hold hard! I'm watching you!

She pulled up, instinctively glancing up. Had he really got his eye on her all the time?

Don't judge others, said the voice.

Oh, all right! said Vivien. If that's the way you want it, I suppose one more scolding won't actually kill me!

She went into the music room, and there was Mrs.

Wright, looking at her watch and fidgeting to be off.

'Oh, there you are, Vivien! I've sent message after message, asking you to come to see me. . . .'

'Sorry, miss,' murmured Vivien.

'. . . and now I've hardly time to explain what's happening, because I've got a woodwind group to take in five minutes time. And why aren't you playing in that, by the way? We could do with that bassoon of yours. . . .'

'. . . well. . . .'

'. . . but that wasn't what I wanted to see you about today. You know that we can't give you piano and oboe teaching here, don't you? Now the Town Hall run a Saturday morning music school for selected children, and I've put your name forward for that. Three other children from this school go there, but they're all much older than you. Your audition is this Friday afternoon, after school. Here's the piece of paper with the details on it. If you pass the audition, they'll take you free of charge on Saturday mornings for piano and oboe lessons. You'll also have to play in their orchestra, but I don't suppose you'll mind that.'

Vivien grasped the piece of paper, and looked dazed.

Mrs. Wright looked at the clock, uttered a small scream, seized a pile of music and said she must go or she'd be late.

The door banged at her heels, and Vivien was left to gloat over her passport to the future.

Wow! she said to herself. And then, after a moment, Thank you, Lord!

Going home, she felt as if she were flying, rather

than dancing along. She hopscotched her way along the road, avoiding the cracks in the pavement. Everything was going to come right, after all.

She stopped short when she reached the front door. Even from outside the house, she could hear the baby wailing, and the noise of the radio in competition with the television set. The Toads said they could do their homework – what little they had – amid all that noise, but Vivien couldn't stand it.

Almost, she turned round and went back to the shops. The public library was open, and there was a quiet section where she could sit and do her homework undisturbed.

Then Vivien gave a big sigh. The Lord had been doing his best for her that day, and it was only right that she should try to do her bit for him in return. She remembered her mother coming in tired after work, and settling down to do some ironing for a sick neighbour in the flats. Her mother had never been idle, and she had always been more interested in other people than in herself.

If her mother had had a neighbour with a crying baby, she wouldn't have walked away from it. Her mother would have walked right into that house and done what she could to help.

Vivien felt a prick of tears at the back of her eyes. Sometimes she missed her mother so badly that it hurt.

Then she thought that her mother wouldn't have wanted her to grow up a selfish woman, any more than God did.

Perhaps she'd better get in there and see what she could do.

Vivien walked into a nightmare scene. There

wasn't anyone in the sitting-room, but the place looked as if a bomb had hit it. Both the radio and telly were full on. There wasn't anyone in the kitchen, either. Vivien turned both the radio and the television off, and shouted out that she was home.

'I'm up here!' said a harassed voice. Penny appeared at the top of the stairs, pushing back her hair. 'Sausage has cut herself rather badly, and the baby's just been sick, and I don't know where the Toads have got to.'

Vivien thought, This is too much! God can't expect me to clear up this mess, surely!

The baby wailed again, and Penny closed her eyes and put her hands over her ears. Sausage also began to wail. From the bottom of the garden came the sound of an almighty crash, followed by angry words from the Toads.

'Oh, dear!' said Penny. 'They're playing at being Daleks again, I think. If they shout "exterminate!" once more, I'll . . . I'll scream!'

Vivien surprised herself. She said, 'What can I do to help? Clear up in here, of course, and what else?'

'You? Would you?' said Penny, in disbelief.

'I can try,' said Vivien, though the mess did make her feel rather faint. There wasn't a single piece of furniture the right way up. The Toads must have been playing at earthquakes, to get this effect.

'Bless you,' said Penny, and disappeared to comfort Sausage or the baby, or both.

Vivien said, Now you've done it, you twit! Fancy offering to help!

She went through the kitchen into the back garden. The kitchen didn't look any better than the living room, and if they wanted supper, someone was going to have to do something about that kitchen first. The Toads were now being SAS men, or paratroopers. Anyway, they were playing with imaginary bazookas, killing anything that moved.

Vivien clapped her hands as she had seen Penny do. She said, 'Boys, we're in trouble. If we want any supper, we've got to sing for it. One of you can help me wash up, and the other had better try sorting out the living room.'

The twins turned their imaginary weapons on her by way of answer. 'Boom! Boom! You're dead!'

Instead of screaming at them, Vivien laughed. She said, 'All right, so I'm dead. And now I'm an angel.' She seized the nearest Toad by one pointed ear. 'And if I'm an angel, I'm leading you to the kitchen sink to wash out your sins. . . .'

'Whoopee!' screamed the other Toad, leaping about like a madman. 'If he's going to be an angel, then I can be a devil!'

'You can say that again,' retorted Vivien, driving them both before her. 'The angel can wash up, and the devil can dry and put away. Then we'll ask Penny what we can do about supper. . . .'

'Fish and chips,' said one of the Toads.

The other Toad said, 'Your piano's arrived, but it needs tuning.'

Vivien looked hard at him. 'How do you know?'

He lifted both shoulders to his pointed ears and let them drop. His brother kicked him on the shin, and muttered, 'You know we're not supposed to go in there!'

Later, after some sort of supper had been prepared, eaten and cleared away, the living room cleared, and Sausage pronounced to be on the mend, Vivien slipped into the study and seated herself at the piano.

Toad was right. The move had caused the piano to go out of tune, but not by much. It was still playable. Vivien felt a rush of thankful tears, as she sat there with her hands on the keys. At last, she thought. Thank the Lord!

Now she could get on with her life in peace and quiet!

Penny opened the door and stood there, hesitating.

'Is the piano all right?' she asked and then, without waiting for a reply, 'Would you like to come through and sit with me this evening? It's so quiet when the twins are in bed and your father's away.'

'No, thank you,' said Vivien. 'I have to catch up on my practising, and then I've got my homework to do.'

'You could do it in the room with me.'

It was the last thing Vivien wanted to do, but in the rush of good feeling caused by recent events, she smiled and said she'd come when she'd done her piano practice. She was rewarded by seeing Penny's face light up.

'It will be nice to have someone to talk to. Baby's been so awful, with her teeth. Usually I go out on Friday nights to my Keep Fit class. Perhaps you could baby-sit for me so that I can go in future?'

Vivien blenched. The baby to her was nothing but a smelly, wailing lump of trouble. Then she thought of what her mother would have done, and said she'd try, but she didn't know if she'd be any good at it.

'I'm sure Dumpling'll give you no trouble at all,' said Penny.

Vivien wasn't so sure about that, but she said

nothing. Besides, she wanted to be in Penny's good books, because of going to the music school on Saturday mornings. Then Vivien remembered the audition after school on Friday, and blurted out that she wasn't sure . . . what time would she be needed to baby-sit . . . she simply had to go to this audition at the Technical College on Friday after school.

Penny listened in silence. She didn't look pleased. 'But what will all this cost? You know I've had to pay Mrs. Kerno a whole term's fees. . . .'

'Mrs. Kerno's no good,' said Vivien, and then bit her lip. She said, carefully, 'I'm sorry I was rude to her. That was bad. But I've apologised to her. What more can I do? I can't learn anything from her, and neither can the Toads. I could teach them more than she can. And you needn't worry about the cost of lessons on Saturday, because if I get in, it's all free.'

'You have it all worked out, haven't you?'

Vivien hung her head. She wanted to get on with her practising, and she didn't know what to say to Penny. She never had.

Penny said, 'Look, I know this is difficult for you. Try to remember that it's difficult for me, too. We'll both have to make allowances. . . .'

Vivien remembered with a start, that the Book had said she must not judge others.

'. . . and I am trying to see your point of view,' said Penny. 'So won't you try to see mine, as well?'

'All right. I'll try. I'll help you in the house when I can. I'll baby-sit on Friday evenings, and I'll try not to get cross with Sausage.'

'Everything's all right at school, now?'

'Yes, thanks,' lied Vivien, and started practising her scales.

9

In fact, everything was not all right at school. Vivien had got herself into the right classes, but she had yet to make any friends. She had made a bad start and word had got around that she was a stuck-up little snob, who thought herself too good for a comprehensive school.

It took time for the other children to realise that Vivien wanted to be friends. She was entering the school near the end of the academic year, when everyone else had already formed up into groups. However, she soon got on speaking terms with the girls in the English class, and the tennis teams. She wasn't brilliant at tennis, but she did try hard, and turned out for all the practices, which made her popular with the Sports Department. For some weeks she refused to go to choir and orchestra rehearsals, fearing questions about the bassoon, even though they were desperate for someone to help out with the percussion instruments.

She found it best to keep quiet when she was teased. Sometimes, when she was cornered in the playground by a couple of rough lads, she prayed for help, and received it. When she showed no sign of fear or temper, the rougher element in the school decided to leave her alone.

In her music classes, Vivien found herself biting her tongue because Melanie seemed to go out of her way to put Vivien down.

Yes, it was hard. But the Saturday morning music school was the highlight of the week for Vivien. It was glorious.

She had passed her audition with ease, and soon found herself hard at work with first-class teachers, who stretched her to the limit. They could see that Vivien had potential, and they called out the best in her. Scales, aural tests, sight reading . . . more and more practice. Soon Vivien was getting up half an hour earlier every morning to get in some practice before she went to school.

At her first rehearsal with the Saturday orchestra, she was told to play third oboe. The first oboist was a brilliant performer, whose fingers flowed up and down his instrument without pause, even when he was not actually playing. He produced a beautiful silvery sound, which Vivien decided she must try to copy.

She knew where she was on Saturday mornings, and after the first month she was on friendly if not intimate terms with two girls at school. She walked part of the way to school and back with one of them. To her delight, Vivien was chosen as First Reserve for one of the tennis teams at school. She felt that at long last she was beginning to make a place for herself.

Even at home, life began to look up. Baby produced five teeth at one go, stopped howling, and became the very model of what a toddler should be. Vivien had somewhat reluctantly taken over responsibility for Dumpling on Friday evenings, and found to her amazement that Dumpling adored her. Dumpling was crawling all over the place now, and would follow Vivien wherever she went – even up the stairs, unless forcibly prevented from doing so.

But the Toads. . . !

One evening Vivien came back from tennis practice to find that one of the Toads was in the study, playing her cherished records. When she stormed in, he was so startled that he pulled the needle right across the record, and ruined it. Vivien picked up the record, and broke it over his head. Then she burst into tears.

So did he. The baby joined in, and all was chaos. Even when the Toad had been scolded and removed by Penny, Vivien sat in a quivering heap, mourning the loss of her record. It had been one of her mother's favourites, a recording of the Elijah, with 'Lift thine eyes' on it.

Vivien remembered how that music had lifted her out of her misery when she had been kept in detention at school, and how it had been a turning point in her life. That piece of music had led her to the Bible, which had become her great comfort in this new life of hers.

Presently the Toad crept back into the room.

'Sorry!' he said. 'Do you want my pocket money, to replace the record? I didn't mean to hurt it. I never did any damage before.'

Vivien sniffed. 'Does that mean you've been in here, playing my records, before? How could you!'

'Why shouldn't I? I like music, too. Why should you have it all, and not me? We're not even going to Mrs. Kerno any more. At least she used to play good tunes for us now and then.'

Vivien blew her nose, and looked doubtfully at the Toad. Her sense of justice made her – reluctantly – admit that he had a point.

'You're the one who likes music, aren't you?'

He slid down on to the floor by the record player. He said, 'I like the brass, but there's something else in the orchestra that I like even better. It's not an oboe. It might be a clarinet, I suppose, but I'm not sure what a clarinet sounds like. I play a tenor recorder at school, but it's deeper than that. There's one on that record of yours that I was playing.'

Vivien got out her record of Britten's Young Person's Guide to the Orchestra. As each instrument came in, with its own solo, she watched the Toad's face. He was totally absorbed. Even his pointed ears were pricked to attention.

'There. . . .' he said in a hushed voice. His eyes were large and full of light. 'That's the noise I want to make.'

Vivien giggled. It was a watery sort of giggle, but it was definitely a sign of amusement.

She said, 'There's a bassoon under the desk here. Do you want a go on it now?'

She put it together for him, and he took it in his big, capable hands, and made it his own. She warned him that reed instruments were difficult to play. He gave her a look of contempt, put the reed into his mouth and blew a long, mellow note.

Then he started to probe for other notes. Vivien got out the Beginner's book on the bassoon, and together they worked out how to produce a scale. Within half an hour, he was feeling for a simple tune.

Vivien sat there with her mouth open, and thought that this was a turn up for the books! The Toad really was musical! What was more, if he was going to turn his quick brain to mastering the bassoon, she was going to have her work cut out to keep ahead of him!

She found she liked the idea of having a musical brother.

Finally he put the bassoon down and rubbed his jaw. Vivien knew what he felt like; playing a reed instrument was hard on your mouth and jaw.

She said, 'Toad, what's your real name?'

'Davy.'

'And your brother?'

'Tom. I thought everyone knew that.'

'What about Sausage?'

'Potbelly.'

'That's not her real name.'

'Fatso, then.'

He was back to his ordinary, horrid self, and there was no talking to him when he got like that. Instead of getting angry, this time Vivien grinned at him.

Toad took the bassoon apart, put it away in its case, and walked away with it. Vivien suddenly remembered that it was not her property. She yelled after him to bring it back, but he took no notice.

What on earth was she going to tell Mrs. Wright?

Vivien need not have worried about the bassoon, because Mrs. Wright had temporarily forgotten all about the missing instrument.

This was all to the good, for it would have taken force to separate Davy from his new-found toy. Davy took the bassoon to school, lugged it home again, and he practised it, using the Beginner's book.

But while Davy was happily involved with producing oompah music upstairs, his twin felt neglected, and turned to teasing Sausage non-stop. Several times Vivien found Sausage curled up on her bed, crying. At first Vivien was impatient with Sausage, but one evening she read the words in the Bible which said you must love your neighbour . . . and if Sausage wasn't her neighbour, who was?

Vivien didn't particularly like Sausage at that point, but when next she found Sausage crying, Vivien did try to help. She put her arm about Sausage. Sausage pulled away. Vivien bit back a sharp word, and tried to coax some sense out of her little sister.

It came out that Sausage was being teased not only by the Toad, but also by her friends at school. They teased her because she was fat and ate so much. Also, she was going to have to wear glasses, because she couldn't see what was on the blackboard in class. Life seemed a grim place for Sausage.

Vivien didn't laugh out loud, though she felt like it. She told Sausage that lots of girls at her old school had been thick set when they were in the middle school, but had suddenly shot up and had got beautiful figures later on.

'But I look so awful!' said Sausage.

It was true. She did look awful. Vivien realised she'd never seen Sausage out of T-shirt and shorts. At her school they didn't have to wear uniform.

'Haven't you anything nice to wear?' asked Vivien.

'I've grown out of everything else!' wept Sausage.

'Then we'll go and ask your mother if she can buy you something really trendy to wear. Something to knock their eyes out at school!'

Sausage sniffed, and said she wasn't bothered. She twisted away when Vivien tried to hug her, but she did go with Vivien to ask Penny about some new clothes. Somewhat to Sausage's surprise, her mother agreed immediately that they should all go shopping that weekend. Penny told Vivien afterwards that she'd been just living for the day when Sausage would outgrow her love of T-shirts and shorts!

Vivien took another look at Penny, because she sounded different all of a sudden. Because Baby was now sleeping through the night and had stopped wailing during the day, Penny was looking a lot better herself. She'd had a new hairdo, and lost some of the weight she'd put on in pregnancy, so that she looked quite different from the untidy, harassed woman whom Vivien had first met.

'I want to thank you, Vivien,' said Penny.

'For what?'

'For being so kind and helpful to everyone. We do notice it, your father and I, you know, even if we don't keep on about it. You're a pleasure to have around the house.'

Vivien blushed and ran out of the room, but she treasured the words, and often thought about them. She'd only been trying to do what the Bible said. She'd asked for God's help to live as a Christian. She knew inside herself that she didn't really deserve to be praised. She knew how often she'd felt angry and critical. There were still times when all she wanted to do was hide in a corner and howl her head off for her mother.

But things were improving.

10

The day after Vivien had decided that things were improving, something awful happened.

It didn't seem awful at the time. Vivien was at the Saturday orchestra rehearsal, and the first oboe player – the boy who was so good – said in an off-hand way to Vivien that there was a vacancy in the Borough Youth Orchestra for another oboe player, and that he'd put her name forward for it.

Vivien gulped. The Youth Orchestra was really good. They gave public concerts four or five times a year. It was said that they were as good as some professional orchestras. Most members of the Youth Orchestra were in their late teens and early twenties, but there were a few gifted youngsters in the ranks.

'Friday night rehearsal,' said the oboe player. 'Seven o'clock sharp till half past nine. Come along next week and play with us. See if you can cope. If you can't you just fade out. Of course, the conductor won't take you on unless he feels you will fit in with the rest of us, but I'll put in a good word for you.'

Vivien swallowed again. It was beyond her wildest dreams, to be offered a place in the Youth Orchestra so soon!

'Concert on the 30th of next month,' said the boy. 'You have to wear black and white, or just black. We get taken there and brought back by coach, but you'll need a packed lunch and tea, because it's going to be a long day. You'll have to get excused from school. We start rehearsals straight after lunch, I think. If your people want tickets, they'll have to get them direct, because I don't think our secretary's got any left.'

Vivien squeaked. 'Concert next month? But I don't know what we're playing! Will I be good enough?'

'You're a good sight reader. We need another oboe to make lots of noise in the loud bits, but you won't be playing in the soft passages, and of course I get all the solos. You should be all right. See you Friday. Right?'

Vivien walked out of the rehearsal on air. But half way home she remembered that she was supposed to be baby-sitting on Friday nights. She also remembered that she was supposed to be playing in a tennis match on the 30th, at school.

From being on cloud nine, she was plunged into despair.

Tears pricked her eyes, and she shuffled her way along.

Well, Lord? she asked. What do I do about this?

There wasn't any direct answer, but she felt calmer when she'd laid the whole thing before him. He'd tell her what to do in due course.

When she got into the house everyone, including her father, was sitting down at table, ready to start the meal.

'Hello, Chicken,' said her father. 'Had a good blow

on the pipes?'

Toad Davy lifted a spoonful of spaghetti and let it trickle over on to the table-cloth. He said, 'Look at my waterfall. By the way, folks, I'm going to start at the music school on Saturdays in September, as well. I asked my teacher and he said, "Why not?" He's going to get me an audition.'

The other Toad kicked at the table till it jumped and made the plates rattle. He threw his arms about and roared with fury.

'Quiet!' shouted Mr. Forrester.

No one took any notice. Penny picked up Dumpling, who'd been upset by the jogging and therefore screamed. Sausage laughed, and so did Davy.

Vivien leaned over and shook Tom. He was so surprised that he stopped yelling, and stared at her.

'Silly boy,' she said. 'Are you going to let your brother steal a march on you? I thought you were going to be a drummer.'

'Shan't!' scowled Tom. 'Music's stupid, anyway! I'm going to try out for the soccer team, when we get to Fairfield.'

'A splendid idea!' said Mr. Forrester. 'Now, if everyone has finished arguing, perhaps we can eat.'

'Well . . .' said Vivien. 'There's just one thing. I'm in trouble, and I need help.'

Everyone looked at her in amazement. She went red. She realised it was the first time in all the months she'd lived there, that she'd asked for their help. She hadn't intended to do so. The words had just come out.

'Yes, love,' said Penny. 'What is it?'

Vivien plunged into her story. How could she go to the Youth Orchestra, if she was booked to baby-sit for Penny? And what about the tennis match? And she hadn't got any black and white clothes for the concert, and she didn't know how to get tickets, and anyway she didn't suppose, she said, that any of them would be interested in coming.

There was a long pause when she had finished. Six pairs of eyes looked at Vivien, and Vivien looked down at her shoes while the food grew cold.

Then Davy picked up his spoon and tackled his spaghetti. 'I'm going to play in the Youth Orchestra too, when I'm old enough.'

Tom said, 'Pass the ketchup. We can all go to the concert, can't we, Mum?'

'Yes, of course, dear,' said Penny. 'We'll get a baby-sitter for Dumpling, and we'll all go.'

Mr. Forrester said, 'I thought I saw something about the Youth Orchestra in the local paper.' He made a long arm for the paper, and turned the pages. 'Yes, here it is. Well, how about that! The concert is at the Royal Albert Hall, right up in London.'

'The Albert Hall!' gasped Vivien.

'Our Youth Orchestra,' read Mr. Forrester, 'has been picked to represent the Borough . . . some kind of sponsored children's event . . . hundreds of children in choirs . . . five youth orchestras. . . . Well, what do you think of that? Our Vivien's going to play at the Albert Hall!'

Vivien nearly died with pleasure and surprise. 'Oh, I do hope they take me!' She clutched Penny's arm. 'But what about the baby-sitting on Fridays?'

'I've been thinking of changing to another night, anyway,' said Penny. 'Of course you must go.'

'And what about the tennis match?'

'You'll have to decide which comes first,' said her father. 'Music or sport.'

'Music,' said Vivien and Davy.

'Sport,' said Tom. 'I'm going to be a footballer when I grow up.'

Everyone burst out laughing, and Sausage pounded on the table with her spoon and fork.

'Silence!' roared their father. 'Let's have some civilised behaviour for a change! Sit down, Vivien, and eat up before it gets cold.'

Sausage said, 'I've finished mine. Can I have some more, please?'

* * *

To get into the Youth Orchestra, Vivien had to play with them at a rehearsal, and then have an audition in the tea-break. It was unnerving. She had to play one of her pieces all by herself, with the rest of the orchestra still in the hall. Some of them talked or drank tea; some listened.

Vivien was scared stiff. Only a few minutes of playing with this orchestra had taught her that they were at a higher standard than anything she'd met with to date.

She closed her eyes for a moment, sent up a silent prayer for help, and then played as if her life depended on it.

When she'd finished, the conductor jabbed at her music. 'There's two beats rest in that bar. Can't you read?'

Vivien looked, and saw that he was right. She went scarlet.

'I suppose,' he said, sarcastically, 'that you're the

sort of player who always come in when there's a dramatic pause, and ruins the effect. I can't be doing with that, you know.'

'No. Sorry.'

'That's all right, then.' He stumped off to have his tea, and Vivien collapsed, quivering.

The boy sauntered over, looking pleased. He handed Vivien a cup of tea and said, 'I thought you'd get in. Congratulations.'

'Am I in? I didn't think he'd take me, after that awful mistake I made.'

'Of course he took you. You sound good, and you watch his beat. He's always hard on us, you know. If he'd decided you weren't good enough, he'd have been terribly polite to you, he'd have said encouraging things about how nicely you play, and then he'd have said he was going to put you on the waiting list. No, you're in, all right.'

* * *

It wasn't that easy, of course, since Vivien still had to break the news to the Sports teachers that she wouldn't be able to play on the 30th. The sports people weren't pleased. Their tennis teams were at the top of the County League and they implied that Vivien was being stupid to pass up a chance of playing for them.

Mr. Bird, the Deputy Head, met Vivien in the corridor and stopped her to say he'd heard about the hassle she was having with the sports department.

'Sorry,' said Vivien. 'But I can't help it. Music comes first. I've been given a permanent place in the Youth Orchestra and that means a lot to me.'

'I understand,' said Mr. Bird. 'Stick to your guns. Mrs. Wright says you're doing just fine. Are you playing in the end of term musical?'

'I wasn't going to bother, but they are so short of people that I did promise I'd go along and help this evening after school.'

Suddenly she remembered the missing bassoon. Mr. Bird had the reputation of knowing everything that happened in the school. Suppose he were to ask about the bassoon? What on earth could she say?

He said, 'Have you heard that Melanie's leaving? I suppose you'll be taking her place in the orchestra next term.'

'Really?' She hadn't heard about that.

He began to move on. 'Remember,' he said, 'I've got my beady eye on you!'

Vivien grinned. What with all those eyes on her, she couldn't go far wrong, could she? But what about that bassoon?

That evening after orchestra rehearsal, she made herself tell Mrs. Wright about the missing bassoon. At first Mrs. Wright looked annoyed. Vivien hastily added that Toad Davy was moving up into Fairfield next term, and proposed to play his bassoon in the school orchestra, if allowed. Mrs. Wright half smiled at that, but then looked vexed again.

'That's all very well, and of course I shall be glad to have a bassoon player, but I do have to account for all my instruments, you know. Officially, that bassoon is your responsibility at the moment.'

'I'm helping Davy with his practice on the bassoon, so that he can get into the Saturday morning college for lessons. Would that count?'

'No,' said Mrs. Wright, 'it wouldn't. At least . . .

you do touch that instrument now and then, I suppose?'

'Well, yes. Sort of.'

'I suppose that's enough to satisfy me that it's in responsible hands, and being made good use of. Vivien, it's up to you to get that instrument, with or without your brother behind it, to the first rehearsal of the orchestra after the holidays. After that, we can adjust our records, if necessary.'

Vivien beamed. It was nice to think about the summer holidays, too, for they were renting a cottage at the seaside for three weeks. . . . Wow! Three weeks to run wild by the sea. . . .

11

It was the night before the Albert Hall concert, and Penny was helping Vivien to try on her new black and white outfit.

With loving care, Penny tied the bow at the neck of Vivien's pretty white blouse, and pulled out the flounced skirt to show it off. Penny had made the black skirt herself. It was long and full, but not too long to trip Vivien up when she went up and down stairs.

Vivien gave a twirl, and stood looking at herself in the mirror. Something had been happening to her figure lately. She was no longer as thin and peaky as she had been. There was colour in her cheeks, and her hair looked glossy.

Penny said, 'I'd like to plait your front hair at the sides, take the two plaits to the back of your head and anchor them there, letting the rest hang loose. That would look pretty and at the same time keep your hair out of your eyes. What do you think?'

'Oh, Penny! I do look nice now, don't I?'

'Yes, you do,' said Penny, smiling. 'I always wanted a pretty daughter to dress up. Of course, Sausage is beginning to take an interest in clothes and eating less, thanks to you. . . .'

'Oh, no,' said Vivien, blushing. 'Not really.'

'It is. I can tell you now, Vivien, that I wasn't happy about your coming to live with us at first. I wanted you to go to a boarding school. I was always so tired because of Dumpling, and Sausage wasn't interested in anything but food, and the Toads were being Toadlike. But you've made so much difference to everybody! I see you keep a Bible under your pillow. Sausage was reading it the other day when I came up to make the beds, and we read a few verses together. Sausage wanted to know why I hadn't read the Bible to her before, and I had to admit I'd forgotten about it. I was always so tired, you see.'

Vivien hugged Penny. 'You must let me help you more.'

'No, you do more than your share already, and you mustn't neglect your schoolwork. Your father says I've been too soft on the Toads and Sausage. We've just got to make them pull their weight about the house, too. But I wanted to tell you, Vivien, that I'm really glad you have come to live with us. I'd like you to call me "Mum", but. . . .'

'I don't think it would come naturally,' said Vivien, with a sting of tears. 'I had my own Mum, you see. Please don't mind too much if I don't call you Mum, I love you, too. Really.'

Penny kissed Vivien's cheek. 'Thank you, Vivien. That'll do just as well.'

Mr. Forrester came in with the Toads, and roared for attention. Penny and Vivien tumbled down the stairs to hear what all the commotion was about.

'Silence,' said Mr. Forrester. 'I have an important announcement to make, and I don't want to have to repeat it three times. Now, are you all listening?'

'Yes,' chorused everyone.

'Then I'll begin. We have just received permission from the Council to have a loft conversion.'

Everyone looked puzzled, except Penny, who obviously knew all about it, and who began to smile.

'Nincompoops!' said their father. 'It means we can put two more bedrooms and another bathroom on the top of this house. Which means. . . .'

Sausage said, 'I get a bedroom to myself again?'

'Yes, you and Vivien get bedrooms to yourselves on the top floor, and also the use of a bathroom. The Dumpling will move into your present room, and we'll all be able to use the bathrooms without queueing.'

'Whoopee!' said Toad Tom. 'Can we have a proper shower in the new bathroom? Can we play submarines. . . ?'

'Quiet!' roared Mr. Forrester. 'Now Vivien, I'm having the rest of my office equipment moved up into a corner of our bedroom, when Dumpling moves out. That way you and Davy can use my old study down here all the time for your music and homework.'

'What about my homework?' said Toad Tom. 'Don't I have as much homework as Davy?'

'You do it here. It's about time you two learned to do things separately.'

Dumpling began to roar. She had been crawling contentedly about the floor for months and rarely cried nowadays, unless she was hungry. Now Vivien saw that Dumpling had actually pulled herself up on to her feet. She was upright, but hadn't yet mastered the skill of walking, and didn't know how to get down on to the floor again. So she roared for help.

Vivien said, 'Oh, Dumpling! Aren't you clever!' And picked the toddler up to kiss and cuddle her. Everyone began talking at once.

'It's a shame,' said Toad Davy. 'What a pity Dumpling isn't old enough to go to the Albert Hall. Then Vivien would have had all her family there to hear her play!'

The Royal Albert Hall was like a giant bee-hive inside. It was crammed with five thousand people, all come to listen to music made by London youth.

There were steel bands, and madrigal groups. There were jazz bands and wind bands. There was an enormous choir of Middle School children, singing a pop cantata. There was an almost equally large choir of boys singing a Purcell anthem.

There were soloists. A lovely girl with a cloud of dark hair sang to the accompaniment of a small string orchestra, and another lovely girl, in a Grecian robe, sang to a guitar.

The orchestras were moved on and off stage with the precision of soldiers on parade. Those not on stage were lined up in passages outside, or sent up to the very top tier, to stand and look down on their colleagues far below on stage.

As Vivien waited backstage with the rest of her orchestra, she noticed that their best oboe player, the boy who had got her the place in the orchestra, was not looking well. He was holding his oboe between slack fingers, and his face glistened white.

'Are you all right?' said Vivien, quietly.

'Help!' he said, in a strangled voice. 'Have you seen how many people there are out there? I feel sick. I'm sure I shall fluff my solos.'

'It's the waiting,' said Vivien. 'It's hard, being last.

I'm sure my reed's going to close up, and I shan't be able to play.'

The lad drew his sleeve across his mouth, and looked as if he were going to bolt for the nearest loo.

'You must have played dozens of solos by now,' said Vivien, forgetting her own nerves in her effort to help him.

'Not in the Albert Hall,' he said. 'My family's out there, expecting me to play brilliantly.

'And mine,' said Vivien. 'And Mr. Bird and Mrs. Wright have brought some of the people from the orchestra at school . . . and then there's the One who never forgets. I'm thinking about him, more than about the others. He knows what we're going through. I'm going to play for him, to give thanks.'

'What are you talking about?'

'You know. "Not one sparrow is forgotten by God . . . even the hairs of your head have been counted". Think of all those people out there as a flock of sparrows, and remember that he knows all of us. Each one. He's always watching us. When I remember that, I know I can do it.'

The boy blinked. 'Are you a Christian?' He seemed surprised.

'Yes. Are you?'

He blinked again. 'I don't know. Haven't thought about God much. What have sparrows to do with it?'

'Don't you know? Jesus said, "Don't be afraid; you are worth much more than many sparrows"!'

'Sparrows, indeed!' said the boy. But he smiled, and his fingers began to slide up and down his oboe again.

'Sparrows,' nodded Vivien.

'Sparrow, yourself!' said the boy, but he grinned. 'I'll remember that. Tell me more, afterwards.'

The signal was given, and they filed on to the platform. It was bewildering. It was daunting. They closed their eyes and then opened them, to get accustomed to the lights. They opened their music, tuned up, and looked expectantly at the conductor.

He raised his arms, went up on his toes, and brought them in.

The players responded as one. They'd practised hard for this night. They'd gone over and over the piece till every phrase was as familiar to them as a nursery rhyme.

They were playing Tchaikovsky's 1812 Overture, with cannon. The music swelled in a glorious melody . . . triumphing over evil . . . praising the Lord for victory over the forces of darkness. Vivien's fingers flew over the keys and her cheeks became red, but she never faltered, and neither did the boy beside her. When it came to his solos, the boy drew himself in, and sent silvery notes flying up to the very roof of that giant hall.

Near the end came the part where they let off cannon. They didn't use real cannon in the Albert Hall, but let off thunderflashes instead. The players had been warned at rehearsal that the noise would be deafening, but that they must control themselves and continue playing, no matter what.

When the first thunderflash went off, everyone jumped in their seats. The violinists' bows jumped off the strings. But no one missed the next note.

They played louder and louder, and faster and faster. The thunderflashes went off . . . bang, bang, bang . . . bang . . . bang!

The hall rocked with waves of glorious sound, and the audience was caught up with it, in waves of thundering music.

When the last chord died away, the cheering began. Vivien stood with the rest of the orchestra. There were tears in her eyes. It had been the most marvellous experience of her life, to play with a big orchestra like that.

She looked out and up to where she knew that her family would be, clapping their hands, and looking down on her. She thought Davy was probably telling anybody who would listen, that one day he was going to play at the Albert Hall. Maybe he would, at that.

The audience did not want to let them go, but now the conductor was giving the signal for them to end the evening with God Save the Queen.

Vivien played from memory, since her eyes were misty with tears. When they stood up for their last bow, she was surprised and pleased that the boy next to her caught her hand, and held it for a moment.

She thought. That's nice. I like him, and he's a brilliant oboe player.

Then she thought. He's going on to University in a couple of years' time, and then perhaps I'll be first oboe player and will get the solos.

She looked around the great hall and thought, I'll be back!

They turned to leave the stage.

'All right, Sparrow?' said the boy.

Vivien couldn't speak. She was too happy. She smiled and nodded at the boy, instead. It was indeed, all right.